M000273667

A Bridge to Healing: J.T.'s Story

To Molly —

Sending love, hugs, and prayers to you during this time of transition. Please remember Kelsey is close by to help. She loves you more than words can say.

Peaceful Blessings,

Darcie Baptiste

A Bridge to Healing: J.T.'s Story

A Mother's Grief Journey and Return to Hope

Sarina Baptista

Copyright © 2014 Sarina Baptista

First edition: Balboa Press 2012
Second edition: Bridge to Healing Press 2014
Edited by Lara Kelleher

All rights reserved. No part of this book may be used or reproduced by any means, graphic, electronic, or mechanical, including photocopying, recording, taping or by any information storage retrieval system without the written permission of the publisher except in the case of brief quotations embodied in critical articles and reviews.

ISBN: 978-0-9912552-2-1 (sc)
ISBN: 978-0-9912552-3-8 (e)

Bridge to Healing books may be ordered through booksellers or by contacting:

Bridge to Healing Press
1966 W. 15th Street, Suite 4
Loveland, CO 80538
(970) 290-9236
www.bridgetohealing.com

Because of the dynamic nature of the Internet, any web addresses or links contained in this book may have changed since publication and may no longer be valid.

The author of this book does not dispense medical advice or prescribe the use of any technique as a form of treatment for physical, emotional, or medical problems without the advice of a physician, either directly or indirectly. The intent of the author is only to offer information of a general nature to help you in your quest for emotional and spiritual wellbeing. In the event you use any of the information in this book for yourself, which is your constitutional right, the author and the publisher assume no responsibility for your actions.

Printed in the United States of America
Cover design by The Incandescent Group
Bridge to Healing Press rev. date: February 18, 2014

For my family—John, ^JT^, Lacey and Anthony. We journey together always aware we are connected in ways we have yet to understand.

PREFACE

I had no idea 71,000 children die each year in the United States alone,[1] leaving their parents lost in what is called the wilderness of grief,[2] with the unnatural task of burying their child. Bereaved parents walk a very lonely and desperate road. In one brief moment, the world loses all of its color. Nothing is ever "normal" again. You join a new club— the "I've Lost A Child" Club. No one wants to join this club. No one wants to walk beside someone in this club. Yet, the numbers are staggering.

The truth is children die.

My family joined this club on March 30, 2007. My son, J.T., died. In that instant, everything I knew about life, death and everything in between fell crashing to the ground and shattered into little pieces. Where is my son? Did he make it to "heaven"? What do I do now?

Through it all, I could feel my son and knew he had to be close! I dismissed the signs he was sending and thought my mind was playing tricks on me. To think my son could communicate from "heaven" was crazy, or so I thought. It was not long before I discovered it *was* my son, and he was very close! I learned how to communicate with him and now work with him every day! He is the inspiration for this book so other parents rediscover their children and transform their lives!

A Bridge to Healing: J.T.'s Story is about the journey back to my son. It is about this amazing boy who worked so very hard to let his mom know he was still very present in our lives and very happy. It is also about the work I do now with other parents whose children are on the other side, and reconnecting them so they can begin to heal their grief.

A Bridge to Healing: J.T.'s Story is also an instructional guide about how anyone can connect with any loved one who has passed. It provides practical, easy to follow steps to reconnect. This is a proven method and is used by students in the Bridge to Healing psychic mentoring and connecting training programs I currently teach.

We are all energy. We are all capable of this amazing connection. We can connect with anyone at any given time providing we are clear enough and minimize our human filters in the process. *A Bridge to Healing: J.T.'s Story* tells how to keep clear and move out of your own way as you practice communication with your loved ones.

My goal and J.T.'s goal is to connect as many souls as we can on each of our planes of existence. Our loved ones are literally only a thought away. It does not end with our loved ones on the other side, either. We can connect with our Divine helpers, angels, guides, and of course, God. Not everyone wants to be a psychic medium like me, but I do believe that we as humans reach for explanations about why we are here and know we are part of a much greater plan

A Bridge to Healing: J.T.'s Story gives hope to those who have had to say goodbye to loved ones, and it gives life to those who have lost their way.

How To Use This Book

If you are a newly bereaved parent, I have a special letter for you in the Resources Section. I suggest you read that first, and then come back to the first chapter.

I also have quite a few references to books and websites which helped me through my bereavement process. All of these are also listed in the Resources section at the back of the book, so please take a look to see if any of these might be helpful to you as well.

This book has three sections.

The first section, **The Beginning**, is about our family's personal experience when J.T. left. It is about losing my precious son and what this did to our family. I learned there is no wrong way to grieve. I share the emotions and experiences we faced and provide tips in maneuvering through the mine fields and surviving those first few months.

I also include how J.T. worked so hard to reconnect with us. There were signs and very clear messages through which J.T. showed us he was still very present with us. I discuss the methods we used to reconnect with him and the process of learning that he was still very much alive!

The second section, **The Answer**, is my journey discovering why he left and what it meant for me. I describe contracts, how I learned I was a medium, my training and my shift into teaching, all with my son by my side to guide me through the wilderness. To have him there and know he was part of my greater plan made my grief journey so much more tolerable.

The third section, **The Bridge**, is the instructional portion of the book. It gives clear direction on how to bridge the gap between you and your loved ones. I address where our children are, the concepts of energy and how to connect with that energy. This is certainly not the only way to do it, however it is a proven method as demonstrated by my students and clients. This is the point at which we must trust we are being guided, and we just need to get out of our own way. The information in this chapter comes directly from J.T. and my other teachers who are with J.T. It is through their clear instruction that I am able to teach you this gift of connection.

Lastly, a **Memorial Section** is included at the end of this section which includes the names of children who have passed, their birthdates and their angel dates. It is my honor to include this memorial for all bereaved parents; our children will never be forgotten.

ACKNOWLEDGEMENTS

I wish to personally thank the following people for their contributions to my inspiration, knowledge and other help in creating this book:

Of course, for the unconditional love and support from my family: John, my one true love and my biggest cheerleader; J.T., my inspiration and source of strength to push me to infinity and beyond; Alessia (Lacey), my mini-me and the most beautiful daughter on the planet; Anthony, my lightening in a bottle who has taught me so much about being a mom and how to live without limits.

Kari Koppes, Denise Regelman and Kate Klusman, for endless hours of watching my children before and after J.T. left, and for all you have done for me since March 30, 2007. You were always there for a shoulder to cry on, a buddy to drink with, and a safe place for my children when I had to go scream somewhere.

My "mommy helpers" Kacie Reed, Ann Pedraza, Kristine Pauplis, Christina Mallet, for holding me, praying with me, and just letting me cry when I didn't know what else to do.

My sisters in sorrow, Jane K., Shirley M., Sue T., Claudia E., Judy L., Donna C., Melissa S., Colleen D. for walking this very unpredictable wilderness with me, listening to me unload and understanding my pain. I know our children brought us together, so I thank them also for the amazing gift of your friendship.

Monika Buerger, Jaime Parrott, Katie Cashman, Faith Rodriguez and Monica Chunn – you are my soul sisters. I surely would have thought I was ready for the mental institution if you were not there validating my experiences. Thank you for the incredible support, and the free psychic advice along the way.

Thank you to my wonderful editor, Lara Kelleher, who continued to edit and provide support even during her own family's crisis and the loss of her mother, Nedra Jones.

TABLE OF CONTENTS

THE BEGINNING

CHAPTER ONE
"We Lost Him"

It is Sunday, April 1, 2007. I never did like April Fool's Day. My husband, John, and I pull into the driveway at Resthaven Cemetery and Memorial Gardens in Fort Collins, Colorado. It is a beautiful cemetery we pass often traveling between our town and the next. I look to the west where the view of the mountains is unobstructed by any buildings or semblance of civilization. It is a beautiful Sunday afternoon.

We enter the building and are directed into one of the family conference rooms. A funeral director enters and we begin the process of determining what our seven year old son would like to have at his funeral. We are burying our child. It would make more sense if it was one of our grandparents, or even parents, lying in the next room, cold and alone. No, we are burying our child.

One of my very good friends, Karen Hawkwood, is sitting beside me. She is there for moral support and to help make decisions if John and I suddenly cease to cope. There are so many decisions to make: the music, the casket, the plot, the program style, the program picture, the verse in the program, what lettering on the programs, how many programs, what our son will wear, what time of the day to have the service, what kind of service, the obituary, the picture for the obituary, where the obituary will run. Our son's cold body lay in the other room. Thinking of him all alone is driving me insane. I suppress the urge to go find him to tell him everything is going to be alright. "Mommy's here. Everything will be fine." Strange thoughts race through my mind—morbid, frightening thoughts about his cute little body and what it looks like now, three days after his little heart stopped beating.

Just three days ago on Thursday, I had my hands full with two children suffering from the flu. I was struggling with food poisoning I picked up the day before and was so sick I couldn't even get out of bed. J.T. and Lacey were seven and five years old respectively. Earlier that week, they both came down with the same virus, same symptoms. We managed to keep my youngest, Anthony, three years old, away from his brother and sister by having him sleep downstairs with John. Anthony was born with a heart defect and I always worry about him when he gets sick. Having three sick children was more than I could fathom at the moment, especially since my own fever and stomach cramps held me close to my bed and bathroom.

Laying there in bed I thought to myself, "If we just make it through the next couple of days, everyone will be healthy again, including me."

J.T. was behaving like any other kid with a virus. He wanted his mommy. At 11 p.m. Thursday night, my fever finally broke and I went into his room to check on him. He said, "Mom, I need you." I said, "OK, let's see if we can get you feeling better." I did what mommies do and found whatever I could to make him comfortable. Lacey was sleeping soundly, for which I was so grateful. Anthony and John had been asleep for an hour or so already. I could devote my time to J.T., who seemed to be struggling more than I knew. He would be fine for a while, almost asleep, then he wanted to move somewhere else. At 2 a.m., he would not go to sleep, so anxious. He said, "Mom, I can't make it!" I was shocked by these words. I asked, "What do you mean, you can't make it?" He said, "I don't know." We left it at that, but those words pierced my heart. I was so weak from my own illness, but I knew he needed me, so we tried to sleep in his bedroom. "He just needs to get through the night," I thought. "Then he would feel so much better."

Exhausted, I lay on the bed next to his. I thought he had dozed off finally and I was almost asleep. Suddenly, he sat straight up in bed and said, "Mommy!" I was startled and scared. I said, "What? What?" He said, "Go to your room." I said, "You want to sleep with me in my room? OK, let's try that." He said, "No, *you* go. I want to watch TV." I was so exhausted at the time, I welcomed the opportunity to sleep, even for just a little bit. I didn't think about how it was not in his character to ask me to leave. I would lay down with him every night. It was our special time together. He would never have asked me to leave his side. At 4 a.m., though, with no sleep and having just experienced food poisoning, I agreed.

I went to my room and slept. I woke up at 6 a.m., which was just two hours later. That's all. Just two hours. I went to J.T.'s room to check on him. He looked so peaceful. I thought, "Ah, he's finally asleep." Instinctively, I looked at his chest and there was no movement. I ran to him and felt his chest. He wasn't breathing. I screamed for John, grabbed the phone and dialed 911. John put J.T. on the floor and I started CPR until the first responders arrived. A Loveland police officer arrived first and took over the CPR for me. The firefighters came next and began their fight to save my boy. The ambulance EMT's hauled all the equipment they could up those stairs. J.T. just lay there. No response. The upstairs was full of men trying to save my son. I started calling people I knew on the phone, trying to make some sense out of what was happening. I was screaming at J.T. to not leave us! I am sure I looked like a crazed lunatic, but I was going to do whatever I could to bring my boy back to me. After the EMTs did everything they could, they ambulanced him to the hospital. I didn't even know the ambulance had left with my baby. I got dressed and drove to the hospital. John was trying to find someone to watch Anthony and Lacey so he could meet me there.

I walked through the door of the emergency room at the hospital and was met by a nurse who ushered me into "the room." This is the place they take you when your child is dying or has died. I was oblivious to all of this in a state of shock and confusion. The nurse, Paula, stayed with me. She seemed to understand. I learned later she, too, lost a child. They knew to send her in the room with me, to have someone who understood and to hold me up.

Then the doctor came into the room. It must have been a half hour to forty five minutes later, although I had no concept of time. Time altered forever from the moment I found my son not breathing. The doctor said they did everything they could, but "we lost him." My mind went into overdrive. What? He's dead? What? How can that be? This is a dream. I swear, this has to be a dream. My baby wouldn't leave me. How could this be happening?

I don't remember much after that. I remember my husband arriving at the hospital. I remember going back to see my son laying on a gurney. I remember stroking his hair and talking to him, telling him how much I love him. I remember thinking I couldn't just leave him there. How do I just leave him there? What mother leaves her son in the hospital?

I remember driving home. John was in the passenger seat reviewing all the pamphlets on death we just received. My focus was to get home to my two babies. What was I going to tell them? How were we going to survive this? I remember thinking that I surely would have to divorce John because I was convinced he was going to go crazy. What am I supposed to do now? Where is my son? The world had turned upside down and we were left hanging off the edge.

A Neighborhood United

June 2005, John and I moved our family across three states from California to Loveland, Colorado. We had no family here, but fell in love with the area. I wondered what would happen now these short three years later. It terrified me thinking how we would be all alone during this crisis with no family close by. Our neighbors and friends came to our rescue, much to my amazement, with a force most people never experience. Even in my state of continual confusion, I was aware of a constant flow of food, supplies, meal sign ups, someone to talk to, someone watching my children and a shoulder on which to lean. Someone was always just a phone call away to come watch the kids while I went and screamed somewhere, and there was always hot food on the table each night. You don't even think about these luxuries during "normal" life. We were surrounded by more love and support than I ever dreamed possible.

Family began to arrive. John's sister, Mylene and God-sister, Kathy and our nephews, Travis and Tyler, hopped in the car as soon as they got the news and didn't stop until they arrived at our door, twelve hundred miles and a day later. I tried to focus on the mundane things, like where to house everyone. It was one way to keep busy and occupy my otherwise defunct brain. Where do I put all of these people? I had no idea. My neighbors came through again. They offered their homes to my family so they would not have to stay in hotels. One couple, Lois and Eric, went so far as to create a "hotel" atmosphere for my sister in her room, with mints and a coffee maker in the bathroom! I was touched beyond words at their warmth and generosity.

Surviving

Tuesday, April 3rd was the night of the viewing. We were not going to go but I realized my children needed to see their brother. They were asleep when he was taken away and Anthony was not grasping the finality of death. We decided it would be good for them to be able to see J.T. one more time.

The whole ordeal was surreal. Seeing my precious child lying there in a casket was a shock to the reality I had created. I had convinced myself I was dreaming and J.T. was just somewhere else. I didn't know where, but he certainly wasn't dead. The proof of my delusion was lying in a beautiful white casket in front of me. Lacey, our five year old daughter, broke down and started to cry. Her pain was excruciating to witness. I could barely handle my own grief but I wanted to take hers away and just have her world be alright again. Seeing him there was just too much for her. I was stopped by a woman named Sandy Johnson I knew from our homeschooling group. I had just found out a couple of days prior that she also lost a child. Jake was four at the time. She told me it had been about nine years since he left. I was stunned she was still walking and breathing. I remember thinking how does my heart know to keep beating when it has been shattered beyond repair? I always thought if you lost a child you would have some kind of mark on you telling everyone of your eternal pain. Sandy had no mark. At one point, I wondered if she was actually lying, because how could she not be locked up in some mental hospital somewhere? How could she still be living and happy?

She said, "I know you do not think you will survive this, but you will. You will survive this." Coming from a woman who was nine years down this road was a huge testimony. I was truly doubting being able to survive life on this planet without my son. I realized later she was sent to save me. I held onto those words with all my being the next few months.

I knew if she could do it, so could I. Whenever I felt myself slipping into that abyss again, not knowing if I was going to ever make it out, I said to myself, "Sandy did this. So can I." I repeated those words multiple times per day, sometimes per hour. They were my lifeline when honestly, I could not find anything else to keep me here.

For those who have lost a child, our thoughts are with that child no longer here. It does not matter if we have other children. Our minds go into an altered reality and we actually believe we must follow our children. We must make sure they are alright. Dying is a very viable option. I was not suicidal, but I certainly was not attached to living, even with two children and a husband still here who loved me and needed me. Our focus is the child we buried. Of course, they need us. A mother will stop at nothing to make sure her child is alright.

Sleep was rare, but when I did sleep, I would dream of J.T. dying again, or of my other children dying. I would awaken in a panic and rush to check my other children. In the morning, I would remember my reality and look for a good reason to get out of bed. I would lie there until one of my children called for me. Truly, they were my saving grace. I would not have left my bed if I did not have two little children who needed to know we were going to be alright, despite this huge hole in our family and our hearts.

I was so grateful for my precious babies. J.T. was supposed to be an only child. It took us a year and a half to get pregnant with him. It was a difficult pregnancy at the end with preeclampsia symptoms and an emergency cesarean. We felt blessed to have a healthy child! Now he was gone. I did not know where he went. All I knew was that he was gone. I did my best to care for and nurture my other two children, watching for their symptoms of grief and getting them the help they needed for their recovery. They needed breakfast and baths and playtime and normalcy. What did that even mean—"normal"? I did my best to make life go back to the way it was before March 30th, but who was I fooling? There is no normal after the death of a child. I wanted it so badly, but I could not will it into existence. My heart was with J.T. I no longer feared death. I just wanted to be with my son. Most bereaved parents will tell you they welcome that time! It cannot be worse than here, living without our children.

Grief Support

I knew I needed help. I knew I could not survive this without assistance. On the other hand, I am very skeptical about "counselors" who claim to know what is best for me. I contacted Hospice, and even though they were very sweet and kind, no one there had lost a child. My world became separated into two groups: those who understood and those who did not. If you had not lost a child, you were in the latter category, regardless of your kind intentions and loving words. This pain was so intense and unpredictable. How could people possibly understand it if they hadn't lived it? That was my belief, and the belief of those in this new club I joined called "I've Lost A Child." I must say that my dear friends worked so very hard to understand. They were there by my side day and night. They did a great job of supporting me, but they couldn't really help me heal. I had to find people who understood. So I joined an online grieving mothers group. It is amazing to me what happens when you share a traumatic event such as this. Boundaries disappear. Countries merge. You become family. We held each other up. There was always someone online to offer a hand out of that swirling grief pit. I got my support and counseling from those who were on the front lines, and survived. I had no idea I would be there someday, helping those other lost souls out of the pit. What made the group work was the diversity of grief stages. There were close to six hundred members in this group— some brand new to the grief and some who had walked the road for years. So regardless of what you were feeling, someone had felt it before and survived. I keep saying this because, as I stated before, we really don't believe survival is possible. It goes against the grain of our being, against the nature of being a parent. All of those questions we have— "When someone asks me how many children I have, what do I say?" "When should I go back to work?" "Will this pain ever end?" "Do I really have to live here without my child?"—only someone who has been through this particular grief understands and can even begin to answer. So many times, it was not even about providing an answer, it was saying, "I know, Sweetie. I get it."

Not all grief groups are created equal. I fell into a great group, but of course there was still drama and misunderstandings. There were many times when I had to take a few deep breaths prior to responding to a post from someone. I had to put myself in her shoes and come from her perspective. This was quite difficult given the gaping hole in my heart. Regardless, we did our best to have love and compassion for each other. I did try other bereaved moms groups, but found it is so difficult to find leaders who had processed enough of their grief to be able to support the members instead of bringing them down. I felt grateful to have such a supportive group by my side as we walked together, not really sure where we were going, but at least we had each other.

There was one exception to my rule about those who get and those who do not. His name is Dr. Alan Wolfelt. He created the Center for Loss and Transition. Surprisingly, the center is located here in Colorado and was only about twenty minutes away. He teaches caregivers and counselors about the different kinds of grief. He gets it! He has not lost a child, but understands this incredible grief. My husband and I had the pleasure of hearing him speak at our local Hospice that year J.T. left. He was the first one I ever heard use the term "wilderness of grief." That is surely what it is, a wilderness. You have no maps, no GPS, and no conceivable way out. These concepts were so important to my healing. He taught me that in order to get out of the pit of grief, you must live in the pit of grief. You must be where you are. Struggling just makes you sink deeper. Denial just makes it more violent. Avoidance just delays the inevitable. No, I had to just sit in it.

8

The Pit of Grief

When I was in high school, there was a pond on the property. We called it the scum pond. Our plan was to throw someone in the scum pond once we graduated. It is so disgusting to us at the time. When J.T. left, I thought about that scum pond and how it had to be better than where I was. I learned, though, the more I struggled to get out of the grief pit, the slipperier it became. Climbing up the sides never worked. Pretending the pit didn't exist only made falling in easier since it would hit out of the blue. No, sitting in the dark, stinky, slimy pit was the only way out. When I would feel those waves of grief crashing on top of me, I would hunker down and just allow the waves to carry me into the pit. Then I sat there. Right at the point where I felt I couldn't take it anymore, I felt the wave lift me up and return me to shore. Sometimes, I honestly felt the hand of God, the Divine, whatever you call that energy, grab my arm and pull me out. I learned I could not offer my hand first. I had to "sense" the hand was there, and then grab it. The hardest part was to sit and wait, wondering if I would survive. I obviously did, but there were so many times I wondered.

Hot Dog Buns

Grief is indiscriminant and has the habit of not giving a damn where you are or who you are with when it hits. The hardest thing I have had to do is allow it to come, regardless of where I am. Take the grocery store, for example. Most of us "angel-parents" have had what is termed a "griefburst" in a grocery store. For me, it was when I went to the store to buy hot dogs for dinner. I was at the bread section looking at the buns. Out of habit, I picked up two packages. I looked at the packages and realized I only needed one. J.T. was not there to eat hot dogs anymore. Like a tidal wave, it hit me. I dropped my groceries and ran for the door. I got to my car just in time for the full force of the wail to hit me. I managed to pull to a remote section of the parking lot and had my screaming fit. My griefburst was over hot dog buns.

I want to assure all who are reading this, you are not crazy. Grief is like an alien living inside of you. You no longer have control over your functions. There is "Grief Brain," which basically makes you feel like you are losing your mind. Again, something has invaded your ordinarily keen awareness and perception. Everything has a dull hue to it, and nothing is retained. Someone could have told you five minutes ago where they were going and you will turn to them and ask, "So where are you going?" as if the original conversation never occurred.

You can also go days without eating. Other well meaning people might try force feeding you, or suggest you see a doctor. I assured all of my concerned friends I will eat when I need to eat. Eventually, I would eat. It was not because I was trying to starve myself. It was because I honestly could not put any food into my mouth. It was a physical reaction to the trauma in my body. I ate when I could, but it was not often. It was harder when was someone by my side saying, "You have to eat something." I already thought I was a horrible parent for letting my child die. I didn't need really need any more guilt to add to that.

The Best of Intention

This leads me into the world of the "best of intentions." No one really knows what to do with us after we have buried our children. Even in the haze of my mind, I remember so clearly something the pastor who officiated J.T.'s funeral said to us. He told us people are going to say really stupid things because they had no idea what else to say. He told us to "love them through it." They really did not mean what they were saying, he said.

At the time I remember thinking what an idiot he must be since we were the ones burying our child and we were the ones who needed the love, not someone who should keep his or her mouth shut. They should be watching for *me*, not the other way around. Not a day later, at J.T.'s viewing, I completely understood what he meant. A dear woman was there to pay her respects to J.T. Her son and J.T. went to school together. J.T.'s passing affected her very personally. After all, my son died from the flu! How does a mother protect her child from the flu? She was terrified. I can see this now. At the time, my pain was so intense I was not paying much attention to anyone else, except my husband and children. She asked me what happened and I told her. She asked, "Did you give him any cough syrup?" I told her I had given him an expectorant to help break up the congestion in his lungs. She said, and I quote, "Well, that must have been what killed him." I looked at her for a moment. Two of my friends immediately jumped between us fearing I would attack her physically.

I am not a violent person in the least, but I suppose they did not know what I would do in that moment. I looked at her with understanding, in that very moment, and I said to myself, "I am going to love her through this." I knew she didn't mean to say that I killed my son because I gave him cough syrup. She was looking for anything that would make her son safe. How terrifying it must have been for her with her only son. My son was in a casket in the other room as a constant reminder of what could happen. So, I loved her through it, as well as many other people who said, "Well, at least you have two other children" or "You'll get over this." When people have no idea what to say because they could not possibly comprehend what is happening, they do the only thing they know how. They speak. God love them.

Our First Sign

I consider myself an aware person. I studied meditation and hypnosis in my early thirties and believe in an afterlife. I had no idea what it looked like, but I had a strong belief it was there. When J.T. left, all of those so-called "truths" went out the window. I questioned everything. Where the hell is my son?

I continued to attend church, angrily, I might add. I had no idea why I would bother going to tell a God who took my son away from me that I loved Him and I knew He loved me. I would mumble obscenities under my breath as I sat there through the sermon. Each time I went, though, I felt a presence with me. I felt someone there helping me. I blew it off as my imagination. It was the oddest sensation. I felt a support and a presence offering assistance, almost saying, "Please let me help you."

Regardless of background, most grieving parents believe in signs. I remember thinking I was crazy to believe my son would come to me from the great beyond and give me a sign that he is alright. Why? Why would he bother? He was off on another adventure somewhere. I remember telling a friend of mine, "It's like he is in school in Europe. I really don't get to talk to him, and he will be gone for a very long time." If only that were true. How I wish I could have just called my boy to see if he was alright. At the same time, though, I felt he was very close. Wishful thinking, I thought to myself.

The definition of a sign, to me, is a message through someone or something to let you know your loved one is near. I know now J.T. was sending me signs from the beginning, but I did not recognize them. My pain was so intense and so deep to my core that it blocked these messages from getting to me, kind of like putting a brick wall between us. The intenseness creates a barrier. We can make it even harder for them to visit if we add guilt, anger, resentment and bitterness to our grief. It is almost impossible to escape these emotions, however. We ebb and flow at the will of the wind, no rhyme, no reason. It is a conscious process we must work through to get past the imminent pain in order to see the sun.

Given all of this, I have a very persistent son. He would not give up. He did not say, "Oh, well, they aren't getting it so I will be moving on." Quite the contrary.

I believe my husband, John, was the first to recognize a sign from J.T. He said it was the night of the viewing, April 3rd. He was beside himself, of course. We had a house full of people who had flown in and drove in from all over the country. John decided to take a break from the commotion and go into our bedroom. He was changing into some more comfortable clothes, and an indescribable peace came over him. He knew at that moment that J.T. was fine, and that he would make it through this. It was just a knowing, a peaceful knowing.

It was a day or so later, when I experienced the same incredible lifting. I went into J.T. and Anthony's bedroom and lay down on J.T.'s bed. It was in this bed I found him not breathing just days before. I was overcome by this horrendous grief and anguish. I started to wail, unable to control myself. The pain was so intense that I did not feel it was ever going to release. I started to hyperventilate, still wailing uncontrollably. I honestly thought I was going to die. All at once, I stopped crying. The tears were gone and I was breathing normally. A bit amazed at what had just occurred, I sat there for a few moments not really knowing what to make of it. I looked up and noticed J.T.'s Mars mobile moving back and forth. J.T. made "Mars" out of two paper plates with some tissue paper at school. He painted it all red and wrote "Mars" on it. It hung from the ceiling by a push pin. There wasn't any air in the room, no wind outside, and no air coming up from the heating and air conditioning vent. I started to laugh a little. I sat there staring in disbelief, wondering if it could really be him making it spin back and forth. It wasn't just spinning in one direction, but it was going back and forth, back and forth. I knew that if there was a breeze anywhere, it would have made it spin in circles, not back and forth. I asked, "Is that you, J.T.?" It started spinning wildly as if it was answering my question directly! "Yes! It's me!" I ran out of the room and grabbed John. "You have to come see this!" I said as I dragged him up the stairs. I took him back into J.T.'s room. Mars was no longer spinning. It was very still. I said, "OK, Buddy, show your daddy what you showed me." Nothing happened. John said, "Buddy, I really need to know if it was you. Please do whatever you did for Mom." At that moment, Mars started rocking back and forth. First, it was small rocking, and then it just kept getting more intense until it was spinning again! We both thanked him and cried. Looking back at what it took for him to make that thing move, I am still so grateful and amazed at my "little" boy.

From that moment forward, I became obsessed with signs. I knew he was there! I knew he was trying to reach us. He was letting us know he was alright! I would go into his room about fifty times a day, begging for him to move Mars. Each time he would! I thought to myself, this has got to be air coming in from somewhere. So I began to test him. He has a dreamcatcher in his room above his bed. A dreamcatcher is a circle wrapped in leather with either fetishes or feathers or both. It is used in the Native Indian culture and J.T. loved having his above his bed. He would tell me in the morning how his dreamcatcher took away his bad dreams. It hung away from the vents and windows. Almost tauntingly, I told him, "OK, J.T., Mars is too easy. If that really is you, move these feathers. Come on. Show me." I waited for what felt like an eternity. I was getting discouraged and began berating myself for not trusting him, for not believing in him. Suddenly, POOF! A blast of air lifted just one of the feathers! It was the second of four feathers. None of the other feathers moved at all! Just that one feather, as if someone blew directly on it. It took my breath away! I was scared and shocked and elated, all at the same time. He really is here! It really is my baby. Thank you, J.T.! Thank you. Thank you for being so persistent and patient with me, as I doubted myself and you. Thank you.

CHAPTER TWO
Is That Really You?

Most of us who have lost kids lose track of time. One day rolls into the next. We are grateful for food on the table and a shower if we can muster the energy. The other very important detail of our lives is to figure out how to honor our children. Many parents take this to extremes, which is absolutely fine if you do not let it consume you. Those who dive into memorials and causes to save other children are so admirable, but I would say to be cautious to not use these causes to distract from your grief.

One of my distractions was the LEGO® Club J.T. and I started together. His cousins, Travis and Tyler, gave him a huge bucket of LEGO® blocks and I gobbled up about $200 more online to add to our stash so we could start a LEGO® Club through our homeschooling group. He was registered at the Colorado Virtual Academy where we met such wonderful people. We would get the children together often to "socialize" for educational purposes. That was our excuse anyway! I just liked hanging around these great kids and their parents!

The LEGO® Club was very successful and a great way for the kids to use their creativity to make "creations" they would share with the rest of the group. I facilitated, but J.T. really ran it. After a presentation of their creation and a picture of them and their creation, all the kids would take apart their creations so the pieces would be ready to go for the next time. For whatever reason, J.T. did not take his creation apart in March 2007, just two weeks before he passed. I did not realize this until I was driven to set up one more meeting in J.T.'s honor. I felt if I did not do this, J.T. would be mad at me for letting everyone down (another very common feeling when you have lost a child). In May 2007, a few days before the meeting, I went to the basement and pulled out the bucket of blocks.

There on the top was his last creation. I began to cry, realizing the blessing of having it intact, but also because I knew he would not be there at our club meeting, and he would never make another creation to share with the club again. I gently pulled it out and set it on the table. I found a display case at the craft store just the right size and we put his creation in the display case so I could take it to the meeting.

The day before the meeting, I went to the cemetery. It was a place I found solace and the ability to release my emotions. After all, who in their right mind would bother a mother throwing herself on the ground wailing in grief next to her son's grave? It was a safe place to scream, throw things, pound the ground and generally cause a scene. Had I done this anywhere else, they would have locked me up. I also escaped to the cemetery to grieve so my children would not have to see my griefbursts over and over again. I am not sure if it was because the club meeting was the next day or just because, but I was truly losing it that day. I fell to the grass in a puddle of despair. That same uncontrollable feeling came over me as it had in J.T.'s room that night. I was falling deeper and deeper into the pit, literally beating my fists on my son's grave when Whoosh! Something just zoomed passed me! What in the world? I thought to myself. It surprised me enough to stop my wailing and pounding. I got very quiet and sat in the grass, waiting.

Whoosh!

There it was again! What the heck is that thing? Was it a bird? No, too small for a bird. Perplexed, I became very still.

Whoosh!

Ah, I see you! What are you doing, Mr. Dragonfly?

There before me was a huge red dragonfly. Instantly, I knew it was J.T.! I knew it was either him or a messenger he sent in his place. I cannot tell you how I knew this. I just knew! I smiled. Still sitting very quietly, I watched the dragonfly with such fascination. I had never paid any attention to them before. Quite frankly, I do not remember seeing them before that day. I'm sure they were there, just not in my awareness.

As I sat there, the dragonfly flew closer and closer, until it was dancing all around me! I began to laugh! That seemed to amuse him even more as he kept dancing in front of me, above me and behind me. I started to cry again, this time tears of understanding. At that moment, I understood J.T. was with me. This dragonfly was telling me my boy was fine! A sigh of relief as the tears fell on my little boy's grave. Thank you, I said. Thank you.

The following day was the LEGO® Club. Lacey, Anthony and I hauled all the buckets into the library's community room, got everything set up, and I placed J.T.'s creation on the table in the center of the room. I told the children we are honoring J.T. today and let's see what we can do this month with our creations. It was incredibly painful to get through the time without falling apart. I did excuse myself to go to the restroom down the hall probably three times to cry a bit.

At the end of the meeting, we gathered all the blocks and carried them back to the car. As we were putting the buckets into my minivan, one of the children (J.T.'s best friend at the time) said something about a dragonfly. His sister was carrying a board with some of the larger pieces that have stickers on them so I just passed it off as a comment about one of the stickers. He was insistent and his sister was not moving toward the car to put the bucket in my van. Again, he said there was a dragonfly on the board. I put my finger down on the board his sister was holding and said, "You mean this?" pointing to one of the stickers. At that moment, a dragonfly which had been perched on the board, jumped up on my finger! In total disbelief, I lifted my finger to eye level so I could see him, thinking surely he would fly away. No. He did not fly away. Instead, he tucked his wings in and looked at me, eye to eye. I started to laugh again. No one there knew about my encounter with the dragonfly at the cemetery. How in the world was I going to explain this to them? But I did! Their mouths, children and parents alike, dropped open as they looked at this dragonfly on my finger. I told them it was J.T., and that he was sending the message that he was with us and he really enjoyed today. Where was this coming from? I thought to myself. The words just rolled off my tongue. I knew they were true, but I did not know from where they came.

J.T.'s best friend wanted to see if the dragonfly would hop on his finger, so we tried it, but the dragonfly had other ideas. He had delivered his message and had other things to do. I got into the car, fighting back the tears. I again thanked my boy for the message, one of many messages I would receive as the days went by. And whether or not the others who witnessed this unusual encounter believed what I said was immaterial! I knew it was true. I knew my son was there, and that he was doing everything he could to communicate with me. That was all that mattered. He was there. He was really there!

As May marched on, we did our best as a family to cope. The neighborhood rallied around us, even these couple of months later. We were so grateful. Many moms on the online support group I joined were not as fortunate. They felt so alone.

Our neighborhood homeowners association gifted us a beautiful memorial garden in our backyard in J.T.'s honor. We chose a crabapple tree for the center. J.T. always wanted one since we lived on Crabapple Drive. The association also chose two butterfly bushes to go on each side of the tree—one representing Lacey and the other representing Anthony. I was not feeling well the day they came to plant the garden. I was still forcing myself to get out of bed in the morning and it was all I could do to get through any part of the day without crying. I stayed in the house most of the time our wonderful neighbors were planting. I did go out to see if anyone needed any refreshments. One of the neighbors helping had written a poem for J.T. about butterflies. It was May now and, yes, there was the occasional butterfly that would pass through our yard and we would say, "Look! There's J.T.!" Of course, we said this when dragonflies went by also since my encounter at the cemetery. I was not prepared for what I saw at J.T.'s new garden, however. Right on the other side of the fence there had to be at least fifty little white butterflies dancing around! I realized later this was J.T.'s way of saying "thank you" to our neighbors for making his garden, including his crabapple tree, a reality. This was the only day they came in such numbers, so it truly was a sign from the heavens.

Here's one of those places in life where you could say, "What a coincidence!" You could say it is wishful thinking believing my son would be able to command a flock of butterflies to dance around his garden to show his appreciation. You might even say that I was looking for signs and would make anything fit into my reality to make me feel like he really wasn't gone. Ah, but I would have to say there are no coincidences! That our loved ones really do possess the power to do this and so much more! Time and time again, J.T. and other loved ones show us they do "come back" to let us know they are fine, and they use butterflies, dragonflies, clouds, rainbows, and other people to get their messages to us. Immediately after someone passes, they are able to do so many things. Their energy is so close to our energy. Their love for us helps create more energy so they can show us they are still here. This is why so many people report seeing or hearing their children and other loved ones immediately following their passing. They might show up at the foot of your bed and gently awaken you. They may hop into your dreams, give you hugs and tell you they love you. They might create shapes in the clouds that are unmistakably them. This happened to my husband just a couple of months after J.T. left. We spend most of our summers sitting in the driveway in our lawn chairs as the kids ride their bikes or scooters, or create sidewalk masterpieces with chalk. The beginning of that first summer was very difficult for all of us. This was one such day when John sat in his lawn chair after the kids headed back into the house. The sorrow came over him. He looked up in the sky and saw a face. As his attention stayed focused on this strange looking cloud, it began to morph. Much to John's surprise, it became J.T.'s smiling face! He immediately ran in to get me, but by the time I made it to the driveway, it was gone. Of course, it was a present for his dad, and meant for his eyes only. We were both very grateful and thanked him for his amazing love.

The truth is our kids will do anything they need to do to let us know they are alright.

Even with their determination, though, there are many things that might keep them from being able to get us those signs. When kids leave, parents will always blame themselves. "What if...?" What if I had taken this turn instead of that turn? What if I took him to the hospital? What if I did not let him stay at his grandparents? He never would have been near that pool. These haunting thoughts are so common. We are angry at ourselves and angry at anyone who might have had even a small part in our children's deaths. We cannot help ourselves, really. It is such an unnatural occurrence that we must find someone to blame, including ourselves. How could this have happened if it was not caused by someone?

There is so much I know now I did not know when J.T. left. If a child dies, they had to leave. There are no ifs, ands, or buts about it. This is a very hard concept to understand when you are one of those parents burying your child. I will go into greater detail about this concept in later chapters. For now, I bring this up because the anger, guilt and grief can keep your child from reaching you.

These emotions are very dense in energetic terms. They are heavy. We can feel how heavy they are when we are in the throes of anger. Imagine a child who is pure energy now working hard to break through that denseness. They work so hard! They know we are sad and that we must feel our grief, but if that grief consumes us and turns to other dense things, it makes it very difficult for them to get to us.

Regardless, they will do whatever they can to get our attention.

I have to say, I know J.T. was working very hard to get my attention because he and I have a lot of work to do together still. I am so grateful for his persistence! I am listing some of the signs he gave us because your child might be giving you similar signs, and all this time you have been thinking it was just your imagination!

One such sign happened Christmas morning. No matter how long your child has been gone, Christmas is just not the same. For years I tried to make up for this by buying lots of presents, but it still is so painful to not have him here in body to share the festivities. This particular Christmas was like the others. John and I were watching the children tear through the beautiful wrapping to see what Santa brought. John got up to get something from the kitchen and I saw something on the back of his shirt. Upon closer examination, it was a handprint! It looked like someone had stuck their hand in flour or some other white substance and gave John a single pat on the back! I knew immediately it was a present from J.T.! Anthony and Lacey both put their hands up to measure the print against their own, and it was bigger than either of their hands, but smaller than mine. I got the camera and took a picture of it since I know sometimes these presents do not stand the test of time. It remained there for the duration of the day and into the evening when we had dinner with John's aunt and cousin. I am still amazed at how J.T. could do that! It was not there when John put the shirt on in the morning!

Another day, we had some friends come up from Colorado Springs to spend the day with us. It was a gloomy day and they wanted to go to the cemetery to see J.T.'s grave. I asked J.T. if he could possibly clear the sky so we could have a nice time there instead of freezing. When we got there, it was still very gloomy and cloudy. As soon as we got out of the cars, we looked up and a wall of clouds was forming. The sky directly above us was clear, but this wall was all around everywhere else. I took some pictures once again because I knew no one would believe me! I knew it was my boy creating an amazing sign for us and our friends. He wanted them to know he was still close by also! I thanked him again. What a great kid.

I know some moms who say to me, "I have never received any signs from my child." I know for that mom one of two things might have happened. First, the guilt might have consumed them so much they do not feel their child would waste the time to come say he or she is alright. Second, the signs the child brought might have been on the subtle side, or they might not believe their little one could have done such a big thing. I will tell you, it has surprised me more than once how these children use energy to get their point across!

The following story illustrates how hard our kids work to get those messages to us. A girl in our town was hit by a car and killed riding her bike one day. She was working very hard to let her mom know she was alright. It was one of those situations where the mom's belief system would not allow the messages to get through. I can totally understand this because her pastor was telling her one thing, and I was telling her another. Who would you believe?

Her daughter was persistent, though! Both J.T. and the girl are buried at the same cemetery, although their graves are clear across the cemetery from each other. For whatever reason, the kids and I stopped by J.T.'s grave. We spent some time there and then turned to head for the car. I noticed an envelope on the ground by J.T.'s grave. It was face down. Some new plots were nearby, so I assumed the card came from one of these new graves. I picked it up and walked over to put it with flowers already there and the name on the envelope caught my eye. It was the name of the girl who was killed! How coincidental, I thought to myself. Knowing there are no coincidences, I pulled the card from the envelope. It was clearly written by a child. Now, what are the chances there is another girl buried in the cemetery with the same name? I put the envelope in my pocket and went to the car.

When I got home, I sent an email to the girl's mom asking if her daughter had a friend by the same name on the inside of the card. A day or so later, I got a return email from her. Yes, that was her daughter's best friend and could I drop the card off at the cemetery office.

I knew it was the little girl trying one more time to connect her mom and me. I thanked her for trying, took the card to the cemetery office and left it at that.

You see, they really do try to get through to us, but we have to be listening!

Signs From Our Kids

Below are some of the ways our kids have let us know they are near. This comes directly from those parents who have shared their kids' stories with me. I am grateful to them for contributing to this section! I include these so you know what these kids are capable of and to be alert yourself for these unmistakable signs!

> Stephanie Johnson: "Tingly feeling on my head and face; a certain picture of Natalie and her sisters that falls over periodically, the TV turning off for no reason, going to a bee themed wedding (Natalie's nickname is Buzz)."
>
> Amanda Eggers Bumgardner: "The smell of a specific body powder (that she used that was *not*

baby powder) when no-one else around was wearing it...I hear the word *mom* in my head (always my favorite one, since Jessica could not vocalize words) but I *know* it is her."

Lynne Scherer: "My daughter changed my cell phone ring tone to Over the Rainbow/Beautiful World by the Hawaiian two days *after* she died which also happened to be her 21st birthday!"

Susan Milam: "When my son, Clint, died we could not stand the idea of his being alone in the dark at the cemetery. He didn't like the dark. So, just before dark every single night my husband would go and put a new light stick on his grave. It wasn't too very long before my husband had to go out of town. He made arrangements with our two daughters and myself to take turns going out there at dark to leave a fresh light stick. I had not been to the cemetery alone yet and dreaded so much being alone out there. But, for the love of Clint, I did it. I got there before dark and waited until the right moment to set up the light stick. Then I got back in my car and lost it....I sobbed and sobbed thinking of my baby being in that box in the ground. As I sat there in my car trying to get myself together I felt a very gentle caress on the back of my hand. I opened my eyes and of course there was no one there. I really think it was Clint saying, 'it's okay Mom'."

Beverly Howell: "My son Jonathan was a chef and I found this "Heart potato" in a bag of potatoes that I wasn't really going to buy, I don't really eat white potatoes but had to have this bag.....this is just one sign that I have received from him....."

Tina Geesey: "I have quite a few signs. The most important one I had was 3 weeks after my son passed away I was babysitting my one grandson.

He was 5 months old. The night before my husband and I had got the boys balloons at a bike rally we were at. Well you know how by the next day the balloons end up on the floor. Well Noah my grandson was sitting on the floor by his crib playing with it. I had to run to the store so I picked him up and went to the store. I was gone around 45 mins. When I came home Noah was asleep so I laid him down in his crib which was down in the living room. I went upstairs to put something away. I don't remember, I think it was tissues. Anyhow I glanced in the bedroom where my son passed and I was shocked. There was the balloon Noah was playing with. It had gone thru the living room up the stairs made a right down the hall to the bedroom where he died and it was around 2 feet in the air and hovering over the exact spot where he had died on the floor. And to beat all it stayed there for 6 hours until I moved it. I feel like he made it stay there so my husband and daughters would be able to see it too and not think I was nuts. Even my skeptical husband was lost for words. Thank you, Barry. He left me it a few signs for the first year but they seem to become much less as I got better if you know what I mean. That first year is so awful. He helped me so much."

Bree Mei: "Our kettle turns itself on at least once a day. But it seems to happen more frequently when I'm going through a bad patch."

Leanna Green: "One day last summer my daughter and I were on the patio having coffee we were talking about my son and how much we missed him. And talking about how we just wished we could see him and no he was ok. A few hours later the clouds got really low and the sky was looking like pop corn puffs it was amazing I went to the garden to work on it my daughter got up with her cell phone taking pictures of the clouds later that night she was looking through them when she found one that you can clearly see my sons face formed through. We sent the picture to the computer. To get a better look and there is no doubt in my mind that's my son. He showed us he was close and he is fine. I have this picture and have added my son's picture next to the cloud picture it is amazing how clear his face came through the cloud. For most they either don't think it's possible or can't see his face but for me and many who lost their child no these signs are real and it is from our children. I believe when you lose a child or children a part of you not only seeks Heaven a part of you is now there. There is now a spiritual side of life we feel and see for a part of our being resides there. And because we search and pray so hard to see these signs they are right there for all that look."

Lynn Walker: "A few months before my daughter passed we saw the film 'Bridge to Terabithia' in which one of the main characters passes over. My daughter passed in circumstances with one major similarity. A number of months after she left us I found one of the cinema tickets in my dressing gown pocket— why I have no idea. Yet a few months letter I saw the DVD in a shop, picked it up, stood in the queue for a while then changed my mind and put it back. Another few months later I picked it up again and this time did buy it. Later that day, I don't know why, I looked at the receipt and then went and found the cinema ticket; I had bought it exactly a year to the day and exactly the same time as the film had started one year earlier when we had seen it together."

Kathy Jackson: "I sometimes get very strong signs that my son is with me. My husband bought me a little gold cross for my birthday last month. I took it out of the little box and was wearing it one day but when I went back to the little box, a dime was wedged in it sideways, nobody can explain how it got there, except my son leaves me dimes as signs. On my first New Year Eve out, a couple of years after my son passed, we check into the hotel and on the bed of the empty hotel room was a solo shiny dime, seemingly calling out to me that my son was there."

Sandra Benson Brown: "On the one year anniversary of Jamie's wreck a bunch of us gathered at the swimming hole/rope swing...we were all planning a Jump for Jamie....a butterfly landed on his dad's hat and stayed from the jump to the water right there on that hat."

Bonnie Mcphail Peloquin: "My son, Christopher, is always letting us know he is here. The TV turns on and off repeatedly on its own when my husband is upstairs watching it in our bedroom. If something is going on that I know Christopher wouldn't like, lights flicker, and things in his curio cabinet where his urn and his special things are start tipping over. He loved the ocean, so my bathroom is themed that way. I have a candle that takes batteries and will makes seagull and ocean sounds when you turn it on. I took out the batteries and I was in the kitchen one day and the candle started going off with the sounds with no batteries in it. He is always doing something to make sure we know he is here. He also goes to other relatives homes and does similar things there too."

Linda DeSantis: "I find hearts everywhere."

Jodi McAuley: "We have had so many signs but the most significant sign appeared the night she passed....I was in my backyard looking up at the sky around 11:30—Midnight and about 10 glowing shimmering birds flew over, harmoniously chirped and left.... so beautiful. She must have been telling me she was home."

Michele Hopkins: "My son Colton was a twin. He fought valiantly against Stage IV Neuroblastoma cancer for two years. I prayed during the last days for he and God to give his twin brother some sort of comfort when he went home, as they were very close. Colton passed at 7:05am on December 5, 2004. Daniel, his twin, was at my neighbor's house during this time because I wanted to shield him from however it came to pass. That day, after our sweet Colton was taken to the funeral home, Daniel came home and we all stayed in the house together that night. Colton was in a lot of pain prior to his going to heaven due to the cancer spreading to his bones and he couldn't walk. The morning following his passing Daniel came into the room I was in and in his clear little five-year-old voice said, 'Mommy, Colton's legs don't hurt anymore!' I said, 'Really baby? How do you know?' He said (very matter-of-factly), 'Cause he's running in heaven with Jesus!'"

Sharryn Swanson: "My son sends butterflies and rainbows as well as 5 cent pieces he also turns on my IMac to play his favorite Eminem songs."

Cyd Ault: "My son died on 10/10. He sends dimes."

Debra Lopez: "On Feb, 27, 2012, I got the news from my older sister Bridget, telling me that my Godchild, nephew Alex 17, was found unconscious. His father went into his room, found him foaming at the mouth. He called 911 and they came right away. My nephew took Zanax, too many--he had been partying over the entire weekend, while his mother was on her getaway. After a few days in the ICU, they had to put Alex into a coma--due to not knowing what drugs were in his system. As a week went by, he was still in his coma with no signs of improvement. When my entire family showed up for support after that 7th day, he had woke up--saying, 'Ricky, Ricky, Sgt. Ricky!' The nurse had asked who Ricky was and my sister said that's my nephew who just passed away July 30th, 2010. Well, when Alex was up, he was weak and told his mom, and my twin sister, that Ricky was with him. He said that Ricky and him were sitting in a white Camero (my son had a green Camero). Ricky was hitting him on his face telling him to wake up and that it wasn't his time to go and that his mother needed him. As this took place, Alex woke up to saying, "Ricky, Ricky, Sgt. Ricky." My husband was Sgt. Ricky--who is my husband. My son Ricky went to bootcamp for the Marine Corp. was discharged for anxiety. The afterlife is real! I cried and was in awe knowing the power that our loved ones have when they pass."

CHAPTER THREE
Coincidence?

C oincidence is defined as "a striking occurrence of two
or more events at one time apparently by mere chance"
according to Dictionary.com. I leafed through James
various books and understood the concept fairly well. I have
had a lot of synchronistic events in my life I could only
attribute to a power greater than me. When I was close to my
thirtieth birthday, I was living in the Bay Area and drawn to see
a man who was talking about past life regression. It was March
1994. I went with my dear friend, Karen, the same dear friend
who held my hand at the funeral home when we were planning
J.T.'s funeral. My father was in the hospital at the time. We
thought it was a benign tumor in his liver. It appeared there
was not anything I could do for him that March evening, so we
drove into San Francisco to see this speaker. His name was
Brian Weiss. For those who know his work, this was before the
Oprah show. Way before! I was excited to see what might
happen! Would I see a past life? Is this real?

It certainly made sense to me. I was oddly attached to
certain time periods and had a very strange experience in Italy
when I was vacationing there with my father, my grandmother
and great aunt. I was in my early twenties. We travelled to the
village where my grandmother and great aunt grew up. It was
about an hour from our hotel. There was a lot of traffic when
we headed back to our hotel, and for some reason, we were in
a rush to get back. We had one set of directions to get there
and back. I remember something guiding me to make a left
turn, like I knew where I was going! My father panicked
thinking I would get them lost forever. We were in a foreign
country, after all, and I took us off the main road! I paid no
attention and just kept driving. Turning here, turning there, for
a half hour, when suddenly, there we were! The hotel was right

in front of us. We cut off a half hour of driving by the detour. It really felt like I knew where I was going. I always wondered if I had been there before. Here was my chance to see. Was I on this earth before?

Dr. Weiss is truly a master teacher here on earth. He led us through a regression and I immediately saw a lifetime from long, long ago. What I experienced was so real, I could not pass it off as my imagination. I felt who I was back then, and I felt how I died. It was absolutely amazing!

The following day I arrived at the hospital to be told my father had terminal cancer which originated in the colon, metastasized to the liver, and he had six months to two years to live, but more than likely less than a year. My father and I had a very rocky relationship. I know he loves me, but he was emotionally unavailable as a father it was very hard to deal with him. In that moment, I remembered what I had experienced that night before. I realized I did not have to fix it. I realized I could work at it, absolutely, but if we did not get it "right" by the time he passed, it was okay. Ah, what a relief! It did not keep me from trying, and my dad and I had some good talks, but he just could not be the dad I needed.

The good news is, we still work on the relationship even though he did pass January 1, 1995, less than nine months later.

Was it coincidence that I attended the Brian Weiss workshop the night before I was faced with my father's impeding death? Not to me!

I can think of so many "coincidences" that occurred after J.T. left. The jargon in my industry is that these events are actually "synchronicity." I had never heard of this word prior to J.T. leaving. Now it means everything. It is the way I know I am not alone and that he is so close I might even be able to touch him!

Synchronicity goes beyond coincidence. "Synchronicity is the experience of two or more events that are apparently causally unrelated or unlikely to occur together by chance, that are observed to occur together in a meaningful manner. The concept of synchronicity was first described by Swiss psychologist Carl Gustav Jung in the 1920s."[3]

Synchronicity is different from coincidence as there are usually more than one event involved. If your child gives you one sign, you might write it off as coincidental. Maybe a song plays on the radio or you see their name on the car in front of you as you drive down the road. You might say, "Hmmm. That's interesting." Now, put those two together – the song comes on the radio and then you see the name! That is synchronicity!

One such incident occurred just a few days after J.T.'s funeral. I was sitting at my desk in my bedroom trying to grasp what was happening to our family. Why? Why did he die? I knew there was a reason for it. It was not a random event. I knew it was not random because Lacey caught the same virus, the same day. Her symptoms were worse— a higher fever and even vomited. This stuff just does not happen without a reason, I thought to myself. My eyes were drawn to my phone list. I just stared at the list. I remember saying to myself, "Someone knows why. Someone on this list has my answer." I thought I was crazy. How could anyone know why? Nonetheless, my fingers ran down the list and stopped on a number. It was the number of my friend's mother, Nancy. My friends Jen and Rob are Anthony's Godparents and Nancy is Jen's mother. I met her twice maybe. I grabbed the phone and dialed the number. She answered the phone. I said, "It's Sarina. Why? Why did he die?" There was silence on the other end of the phone for just a moment. Then she said, "It's funny you should call because J.T. visited me last night and he has a message for you. Grab a paper and a pen, you need to write this down."

I obeyed immediately. She told me the message from J.T. who came in a dream to her:

> I did not want you to see me leave.
> You were the perfect mom. You did everything perfectly
> I had to go. I tried twice before to leave but I could not leave you. This time I had to go.

After I wrote it out, I began to cry. She said, "You know, J.T. loves you very much and he still spends time with the family." Right then, something caught my eye on my desk. I looked down and saw a little slip of paper. I picked it up and it read, "I love you, Mom. J.T." It was J.T's handwriting, but I have no idea from where it came. I was stunned! How did he do that?

Synchronicity also led me to discover my gifts. Still searching for answers, the only person who might be able to help me was Brian Weiss. I had not thought about Brian Weiss for at least a decade, but my son had just died and I needed to know more. I thought if anyone had answers, it would be Brian Weiss! I began searching his website. His next workshop was going to be in Seattle, Washington in November 2007. It was only July 2007. I knew I could not wait until November. A little more research revealed he was doing this workshop with another author—a man named John Holland. He apparently was a psychic medium. His latest book, *Power of the Soul* had just been published. I was intrigued. I had never been drawn to read anything from psychic mediums before, but I thought if he was good enough to be on the same stage with Brian Weiss, he was good enough for me to check out. Switching over to his website, I found he was going to be coming through my town in just a couple of months! I knew I had to go, so I immediately bought two tickets to his appearance and his new book. I figured I'd better learn a little about this guy before I go see him. This was a brand new world to me. I wanted to be armed!

By the beginning of September, I had decided maybe a reading from a medium would be in order. I had received enough signs from J.T. at this point to know he did not really die. Some part of him lived on. I was in a totally unfamiliar world and I knew that maybe if I could talk to him through a medium, I would understand more about this whole thing. I made an appointment with a medium in California who was recommended to me by my friend, Jen. Her name is Michelle Oborny. At the same time, I began reading John Holland's book, *Power of the Soul*, to become familiar with his work before his event at the end of the month. I remember distinctly reading the chapter on clairsentience, which is how you feel those on the other side. At the end of the chapter, John has some bullet points labeled "You might be clairsentient if…" I remember reading the points and immediately a light bulb went off in my head! I said out loud, "I can do this!" I was stunned as the words came out of my mouth. What did I just say? That I could talk to dead people? Oh my God. I really have lost it.

That day I met my friend Karen for lunch. She had been on this rollercoaster with me since March 30th and April Fool's day at the funeral home. I figured if I was looney bins, she would tell me. I told her about what I read in the book and how I think I found out what I was supposed to do with this. Could it really be that? I mean, who does that, anyway?

After our lunch I stopped at the store. One of the signs you are clairsentient is when people stop you in stores and ask you where things are as if you are an employee. I have no idea why that would be, but it has happened to me more than once. John in his book and at his workshops uses the example of being at a carpet store and a lady asking him to help her choose her carpet. She obviously thought he worked there by the way she spoke. I laughed when I read this part of the book since I have had these experiences. I got a motorized cart at the store that day because I broke my toe a couple of days prior and it was just so painful to walk. As if on cue, I am in my motorized cart looking at toothpaste when an older lady says to me, "Excuse me. Where are the curlers?" I turned around and she was just standing there waiting for my answer. I expected her to say, "Oh, you do not work here." No. There she stood, intent on my answer. I know the store's layout fairly well, so I confidently said, "One aisle over." She thanked me and went on her way. I burst into laughter! There I was, in a motorized cart, and she thought I worked there. I said, "OK, I get it!" I knew I was not dreaming at that point. I was given my answer very clearly.

This is synchronicity. Two days later, I had my reading with Michelle who confirmed I was clairsentient, meaning I could feel when spirits are close to me.

This particular synchronicity did not stop there. That winding road led me to see John Holland at the end of September where a local medium came on stage first. I felt so badly for bringing my husband to this "freak" show, as I termed it then. By this time I was enrolled in a class at the Psychic Horizons Center in Boulder, Colorado, about an hour away. I was happy to make the drive since it meant learning how to communicate with J.T. I still did not understand very much about where he was. It was great watching John as he received messages for loved ones in the audience. I had never seen anything like it! As I mentioned, a local medium opened for John. I could feel J.T. was very near. I just wanted to know he was okay. I got very nervous as the lady on stage started describing my son. John and I looked at each other, still not believing our little seven year old boy could possibly be able to participate in this. Then she said, "The name 'Buddy' is important." I knew at that moment, it was J.T.! We've called him "Buddy" since birth just as another nickname. We raised our hands and stood up. I was shaking so badly and crying, I could barely remember what she was saying. Some dear soul in the audience was writing it all down unbeknownst to us. I'm so thankful for this since it is just a blur. For anyone who has received a reading from a loved one like this, it is very unnerving!

After the reading, I was looking at the material in my lap I received when we walked in the door. There in front of me was the name of the local medium and information on a psychic workshop she was having in a couple of weeks. I guess J.T. wants me to go?

At the end of the show, I went to the restroom and the local medium was speaking with some other audience members. I stood there for a few minutes waiting for my turn to talk with her. I thanked her for giving us messages from J.T. She told me he had actually came to her a couple of days prior and told her who we were and where we would be sitting. Determined little boy! It was the first time I realized how important it was to J.T. that I get these messages, that I understand where he is and what he is doing now. I still could not believe I was going to be able to talk with him. It seemed so far away. I also knew, though, that he would make sure it happened. I trusted that.

Looking back on how each step took me to the next, I am still amazed at how he got me to where I was. How did he do that?

It is so easy for our minds to discount synchronistic events. Just as with signs, we think our angels could not possibly do what we just saw or experienced! Think again! They can and do.

As difficult as it is sometimes to believe there is a plan, especially after you have lost a child, believe me when I say there is. More than that, your child wants to connect with you and wants you to know he or she is doing just fine. I have included some exercises in this book to strengthen that connection with your child, but before you do this, start looking for those "coincidences" and synchronicities. Write them down in a journal, whether you truly believe they are or not. Write them down anyway. You will be amazed at how many you have!

I would also say to be choosy to whom you speak about these events. We have very well meaning friends, especially when we have endured such a loss. Many do not know what to do with us. I cannot tell you how many grieving moms with whom I have spoken who say their friends tell them it is just their imagination when they believe they receive these signs. Despite the good intentions, this can be very detrimental to your healing. Why wouldn't your child come back and let you know he or she is okay? For some, though, this is very threatening and whether they realize it or not, they tend to fall back into that place of fear when they are presented with events they deem out of their control. More than one person told me, "Oh, sweetie, whatever you need to do to get through the grief" symbolically patting me on the head when I told them I could hear J.T. Do not let these people deter you! If you even vaguely feel this is from your child or the sequence of events means something, write it down! Then say "Thank you" because your child is working so very hard to get that message to you!

THE ANSWER

CHAPTER FOUR
Did I Agree To This?

From the moment the doctor at the hospital told us our little boy was "gone", I knew there was a reason. I knew it was not a random occurrence and, well, just live with it. I have always been inquisitive. I have always asked "Why?" Growing up in a Catholic school environment, I asked why. Why do I need to tell the priest my sins to be forgiven? Why would this God be so mean to animals to not let them into heaven? Why did I have to sit in Church every Sunday to be a good person?

Most of these questions I could not voice, of course. My mother and father were very wonderful to not force any religion on me. They got divorced when I was eight, so the Catholic Church excommunicated them. That meant they were not allowed to have Communion, the most sacred of the Catholic sacraments. I thought it was odd that God would punish two people for not being able to get along. Rather harsh, I thought. It did not make much sense to me at the time, but, of course, not much in my world did make sense. I chalked it up to another one of those "crazy world in which we live" things.

When I was seventeen, my step-brother Don died. That same year, one of my cousins died, and a fellow classmate died just a couple of months after my brother. My world was really shaken, but through it, I found something I was not expecting. It was my first encounter with God – the loving God I knew existed but no one could tell me where he was. My brother's motorcycle accident happened the Wednesday before Thanksgiving. The following Tuesday, he was taken off life support and died. Strange things during happened that week. Looking back on it, I see what my brother was doing, but at seventeen, I had no idea what was happening. Don came to me in a dream. He told me he was alright and to not worry about him. The entire time we were talking, I could see a shadow of a figure behind him. I knew it was "God." They walked off together and I knew my brother was going to be alright wherever he was. Two days later, I was crying driving to the hospital. It was a partly cloudy day. Something caught my attention in the sky and I looked up. Sitting there at a stop sign, the most incredible feeling of peace and love came over me. For those of you who have experienced this, you know what I mean. It is the same peace and love J.T. gave me in his room that night, and another time at church shortly after he left. There in that moment, I was happy. It had been a long time since I had been happy. It was such a beautiful feeling! I got to the hospital, of course, and was not able to maintain that feeling, but I surely remembered it.

Don's hospital room in ICU had a very distinct smell. I would drive home at night after visiting with him and I would smell that smell in my car, so strongly. It took a few times for me to catch on. It was my brother letting me know he was there.

When my classmate died a couple of months later, it threw me back to that place of grief over my brother. I had two very dear friends at the time, Colleen Bray and Lisa Denise Marshall (now Tuemmler) who rode the wave with me during that time. Colleen came to my house so we could drive together to our classmate's funeral. I approached the car and stopped in my tracks. The windows were all fogged up. I hadn't driven the car for a few hours; the weather was standard for Southern California. I got in and realized they were foggy on the inside, not the outside! Then the smell hit me! It was my brother! I told Colleen, "Don's here with us, and he will be coming to help us." She gave me that look like, "OK, I don't know how to respond to this since I think you are nuts, but I will just nod my head." I felt safe. Don was there.

A month or so later, I hit a wall of depression. It is hard enough being seventeen without all this death around me. I really did not understand the purpose to living. It seemed so pointless. We grow up with pain and hurt, and then we die. I did not see much in between. I drove my car up the mountain road. My intent was to find a curve on a very high cliff and put the pedal to the metal and go out with a bang!

Something very strange happened to me as I was driving up that mountain road. I heard in my head, "If I do this now, I will just have to come back and do it over again!" I thought, now that is odd. What the heck does that even mean??? I pulled off the road and parked for a few minutes. I heard it again. If I do this right now, I will have to come back and do this all over again. My immediate thought was "Oh hell no! I am *not* doing this $h!t again!" I had no idea where the thought came from and I wasn't sure if it was even true! It was enough, though, for me to turn the car back around and go back down the mountain.

Catholics don't believe in reincarnation. I didn't know one way or the other. I always left it open in my mind that maybe it could happen. I felt very connected in my life to certain time periods I would learn in history class, and I felt I had been here before, but it never really came into my awareness until that day.

Somehow, I recovered. When I would think about ending my life, I remembered that day on the mountain.

Did I agree to this?

I mentioned before there were so many synchronicities leading me those first few months after J.T. left. Searching for Brian Weiss and finding John Holland; reading John Holland's book discovering I was a medium; going to John Holland's show to meet others who would take me to the next step. I stumbled on another piece to the puzzle when I was researching past lives. I knew what it felt like to be in other lives through the regressions with Brian Weiss. Then the phrase, "Life Between Lives" popped up in a search I was doing on the internet. Life between lives? What in the world was that? Doing some further research, I found the site of Michael Newton, Phd. He wrote a couple of books about the Life Between Lives. In the description, it is the time we are in the Spirit world and are choosing our next life. I was certainly intrigued since I was told by a few people by this time that J.T.'s death was a contract and I agreed to it. I looked at each of them with that same look Colleen gave me back when I was seventeen. However, I knew enough at this point to know I needed to follow the lead. I got the book, *Journey of Souls, Case Studies of Life Between Lives*. I was reading this book when we made our trip to California in July 2007. That was a hard trip. We were going back to see family and it was important to me to show them we were doing alright. I was not doing alright. My family was not doing alright, but I forced it anyway. I definitely would not recommend this. Of course, at the time, I thought I was helping the situation, but I honestly was not being true to my grief.

Driving through Utah and Nevada, I am reading this book. So many things in *Journey of Souls* resonated with me. It felt right and filled in more of the puzzle. The premise is that we all get to choose the life we are in right now. We get to choose our appearance, our parents, our siblings, our mates, and our children. I thought to myself, "Is this the contract I kept hearing about?"

The concept was so foreign to me. How does a mother agree to have her son die? Ludicrous! What could I possibly have to learn to endure so much pain? Why would I do this? Why would we all agree to this?

Still, the book made a lot of sense to me. I knew there was more I needed to learn from this. From my hotel room in California, I got on the internet and started looking for trained therapists to do this "Life Between Lives" regression on me. I am a very good subject for hypnosis. I can go very deep, very quickly. I needed answers, and if this was the way to get them, then I was going to do it.

I found a woman who lived about forty-five minutes from me in Colorado. Her name was Linda Backman. I immediately called the number on her website. Both the website and the voice message said the wait for an appointment was around six months! I took my chances and left a message anyway. I needed to know **did I agree to this?**

Within the hour, Earl, Linda's husband called me back. They just had a cancellation for August 6th. That was only a week away! I thanked J.T. for getting me the appointment. I knew it was him. He knew his mom needed some answers.

40

The following day, we visited our family chiropractor there in California, Monika Buerger. She was very close with J.T. She told us he visited her often, that he would help her get through the tough days. I was so jealous she could see him and talk to him. I wanted to be able to do this also! He told her he had big plans for me. I screamed, "WHAT? What are these plans?! I need to know." Soon, he told her. Soon.

Looking back again, he knew exactly who to give messages so I would follow the path I needed to follow. He knew who I trusted. Honestly, whoever had a message from him, I was an eager listener, but I did not always believe what everyone said. Monika I believed. I could feel it in my heart. I knew there was a reason for all of this. I knew it. I knew I was supposed to do something really big, but I had no idea what. I already felt I would help other bereaved parents with my story and help them walk through the wilderness, but there was more. I knew there was more.

Those days leading up to August 6th were agony. I wanted so much to figure this all out. I was tired of where I was. I knew I needed to grieve, but I also knew I needed to do something more.

Finally, it was here. I drove to Erie, Colorado to Linda Backman's house. We began talking and the first light bulb moment was when she told me she had a miscarriage. She went into counseling to help other parents go through this type of devastating loss. She knew my pain. I trusted her instantly.

We began the series of regressions to get me to that "between life" place. It took all day to get there. Each regression took me deeper and deeper into hypnosis. I felt distracted and not getting as much information as I had in my regressions with Brian Weiss. I was getting frustrated, to say the least. She reminded me of the trauma I endured just a little over four months prior. I was asking a lot of myself to get through the distractions and get to that place I wanted so much to see.

Suddenly, I was there! I came out of the lifetime and my guide met. He said, "Welcome home!" We started walking together and in the distance I saw a large group of people. I knew they were souls, but they looked like people since that was my only frame of reference. We were very close to the group when one person broke out of the group and began running to me. It was J.T.! I was so happy to see him and I started to cry. She asked me what was happening. It was hard to answer her questions; I was concentrating so much on just hugging my boy. I realized that this encounter was really happening. It took me by surprise as I was expecting to see what happened after that life I just left. Instead, they brought me to current time. I recognized others as members of my soul family, although I did not know who they were, really. One very peculiar thing did happen. My dear friend, Karen, was there. She always calls me "sweetie". She came up to me and patted me on the back and said, "You are doing great, Sweetie!" I knew it was her, but she is still very much alive! I would learn later more about why she was there. Right now, I was with my boy, and nothing else mattered.

My guide, J.T. and I separated from the group. Linda asked me to ask them what I wanted to know. I asked, "Did I agree to this?" J.T. took my hand and suddenly I was back in that place, the place where we were all sitting around this table. John was there, Lacey was there, Anthony was there, I was there and J.T. was there. I saw us talking about the life we are currently in and what needed to happen. I saw myself saying, "Yes, that's what we need to do."

There it was. I did agree. As I was watching this play out, I remembered being there. The memory was so clear. It was too soon to know why this all had to happen, but I did say I would do it.

A part of me was very relieved that day, and a part of me hated me for agreeing to this nightmare. The experience between lives was very real. Some might say it was projection or imagination or whatever. I know it was real. To this day, I can still see J.T. running to me and jumping into my arms. In a strange way, it lifted some of the burdens of grief. Knowing there was a plan and that I was not just a victim to circumstance helped me move forward in my journey and break through some walls others face along this rocky road. I saw my son. I knew he was okay. I know I'm not crazy.

A funny thing happened about two months later. One of J.T.'s friends' moms called and said, "We need to get together." I was happy to reconnect with her! Margaret is a beautiful soul and I had not talked with her much in the previous six months since J.T.'s funeral, but I knew she was there if I needed to talk. We met at a Mexican restaurant and she told me J.T. had really been on her mind. She knew she had to reach out to me and tell me some of the things she had experienced. She began to talk about this crazy book about the time we spend between lives. She leaned in and said softly as if she did not want anyone to overhear the secret she was about to reveal, "You know, I saw this woman in Erie and she hypnotized me and I went to that place between lives!" I burst into laughter; I had not met a soul up to that point who had even heard of such a thing, and there in front of me was another person I knew who went to Linda Backman! She said, "I know it sounds crazy." I interrupted her and told her about my experience in August. We must have laughed for fifteen minutes! Once again, the Universe brought me someone to validate that event. What an absurd idea, that life between lives thing! Yet, my experience was very real and I know to this day it was a true experience.

So I agreed. What now?

Did You Know You are A Medium?

As anyone who has lost a child can attest, life is a day to day survival. You wake up in the morning, praying you can get through the day so you can go back to bed. You hope you sleep, but you don't know if you will or not. Will the nightmares return? Those dreams of your child in danger or in peril and you can't get to them. You watch helpless as your child dies again. Or the dreams of your other children being murdered or kidnapped or some other horrific event that separates you from your child. I do not know of any grieving parent who has not experienced at least one of these.

After seeing my son in the between life state, I had an added fear. What else did I agree to? What other tragedy was going to befall my family because I agreed to something I don't remember? Any parent will tell you the fear of another child dying is overwhelming. I would check to make sure my children were still breathing at least five times each night.

There was nothing physically wrong with them. That didn't matter, though. I had a healthy son die in my care. What would stop another child from dying in my care? Nothing.

For many parents, these fears take over their lives. They live and breathe in fear and terror. It overwhelms them to the point they are in a constant state of anxiety. I understand the need for medications to help cope with their new reality, although I knew from the beginning I could not take that route. I had to face this with all my faculties intact. Looking back, I am glad I did. The road I was on was going to get crazier and even more out of this world. Had I been on medication, I would surely have thought I was hallucinating.

The words my dear friend, Monika, said to me kept ping-ponging in my head. She told me, "J.T. has big plans for you. I don't know what they are, but they are big!" I prayed she was right, that there was going to be something to come out of this to make it "worth it." Nothing really would make it worth it. That is almost ludicrous to say. We all hope, though, something will come out of our child's death to prove to us there really was a bigger plan. I held onto my friend's words, and I was determined to find my "why."

In the last chapter I wrote about synchronicity and how I would jump from stone to stone laid in front of me. As I wrote in that chapter, one of those leaps of faith led me to the medium, Michelle Oborny. This was one of those encounters you dream about having, where suddenly, order is restored to the chaos. I will never forget that day. I was so nervous. The minutes were counting down until she called me and I was so nervous. I had never spoken to a medium before. I went to a palm reader once, but this was so different. There's nothing like having a child die to force you to look at all of your beliefs and take you into territory you would never consider viable before.

My heart was in my throat as the phone rang. Michelle was so caring and loving. She knew nothing about my son or why I wanted a reading. She explained her process. She had meditated on what the guides wanted to tell me and that is how she is so clear about things. I tried to concentrate on what she was saying, but my thoughts were bouncing around so much, and I found I had to keep bringing my attention back to what she was saying. I was begging J.T. to tell her something. Instead she said, "They are showing me a contract." "They," she explained, were my guides – those helping me in this lifetime with what I had to do here. She asked, "Are you buying a house?" I said no. She asked my guides more questions about the contract. She told me, "It is very thick ink, like this is a very important contract." Then she said, "Oh, I understand now. They are showing me *your* contract. They say you have agreed to this contract and it is very important that you fulfill it. They are emphasizing how important it is and how thick the ink is. You must do this, they say." I was a bit bewildered, but I recalled my encounter with the lady in at the store and John Holland's *Power of the Soul.* I could not believe that was what she meant, so I kept quiet. Almost as if on cue with the question in my mind she said, "Did you know you are supposed to do this, too? You are a medium and you are supposed to do what I do?" I was silent for a second. The enormity of her words hung in front of me. Could it be, I thought? Was I really hearing what I think I am hearing?

She interrupted my inner chatter by saying, "They say you can hear them." I immediately said, "No. No, I cannot hear them." In my head at that very moment I heard words, which were not mine. "Yes, you can. You can hear us." I said, "OK, I guess I can hear them because they just told me I could."

At that moment, my world changed. The color and texture of everything around me shifted. I was seeing it all through different eyes. That dark curtain that followed me around since March 30, 2007, was raised. I could see so clearly, it was almost frightening. I asked, "How do I do this? How do I learn to do this? What is the next step?" Michelle replied, "Training. You must get training. That is imperative." I agreed. How else would I possibly be able to do this?! I was suddenly in this alternate reality. The prospects of it intrigued me. On the flipside, I was terrified!

We talked a bit more about what kind of training and where I should go from there. She told me things about the future – what would be happening for me in a couple of years and gave me some ideas about what to expect. I took them with a grain of salt, of course. I could barely see the next day in front of me, let alone a couple of years! At the end of that conversation she asked, "Is there anything else you would like?" I said, "Yes. I want to talk to my son." There was a pause. Then she said, "I am smelling….something like dirty socks. Very smelly!" I was stunned! I said, "Oh my God! That's what that is? I thought I was going crazy!" Since J.T. left, I would go into his room and smell his dirty laundry! I was always on him about putting his clothes in the hamper. Phew, did they smell! For a seven year old, they stunk! The day after J.T. passed, a dear neighbor took all of his dirty clothes, hamper and all, and washed every single article. I searched high and low for that missing underwear or sock that was left under the bed or in the closet. I couldn't find it! Yet, the smell was so powerful! It all made sense. If there was one smell that would identify it was J.T visiting, that would be it! I knew J.T. was a powerful little soul, but I had no idea they could do things like this! Michelle told me things about that night before J.T. left and some things surrounding his death which made the picture clearer for me. Such peace of mind! I was so grateful to have answers! I have a good sense when someone is telling me something true and not true. This was definitely true information. I was so relieved. In that moment, it was hard for me to comprehend I would be doing this for others.

She said, "J.T. says you are the bridge between his world and yours, bringing other families back together and connecting them with their children on the other side." WOW! I would say my friend Monika was right! Those *are* big plans he has for me!

CHAPTER FIVE
So You Say I Can Do This

September 2007 was a turning point for me. Yes, I still had to grieve—there was no escaping this. I had purpose and direction, though, that was not present in my life in August. It was a short five months since J.T.'s passing, but it felt like an eternity to my soul.

The month began with my reading with Michelle Oborny. At the end of the month, I attended the live event with John Holland and met the medium who brought J.T. through. Right there, in front of six hundred people, J.T. was telling me he was very much still alive and had great things ahead for us. This medium had also lost a child, which J.T. knew was so important to me. Only those who have had this type of loss understand it. I needed that connection so I would trust her. I did trust her.

I began my training in October 2007. We had just passed J.T.'s six month angelversary and I was training to be a medium. I did not know at the time how quickly I was opening to receive from the other side. I distinctly remember waking up in the morning and being able to do "things" I could not do the evening prior. Such was the case in reading people's energy. I awoke one morning and suddenly I could feel other's feelings and I could hear what they should be doing. Just like that, I was psychic.

I took my training seriously. I remembered Michelle saying how important training was to my fulfillment of my contract. I also took classes, as I said before, at the Psychic Horizons Center. I was so afraid I would find I really could not do this work – my fear was I would be labeled a fraud and incapable of receiving anything more than just feeling when J.T. was around or smelling his dirty socks.

November 2007 would change that. I had my first visit from someone other than J.T.

One night while I was in bed, I felt the vibration. It actually woke me up! I asked J.T. why he would wake me up like that! He should know I needed my sleep! I told him I loved him but he needed to go away so I could sleep.

The following night, the same thing happened. It was about midnight and I was awakened by this vibration in my body. By this time, I was getting a bit irritated with my son. "What, J.T.?! What?! What do you need that is so important it cannot wait until morning?!" He was still my son, after all, and I felt entitled to ask him what he was thinking waking up his mom! I realized, or was given the thought, that it was not J.T. I felt a little scared. This was such a new life for me and I was clueless how to handle it. I couldn't hear whoever this was, and he wouldn't leave me alone!

The following day, I called my mentor and explained what happened. We both tuned in and I actually got the message! It was my first encounter with a spirit I didn't know! I felt so accomplished and so excited! Spirits were coming to me and I was getting it! This must mean I really am a medium!

I think before this event I had high hopes I could learn how to do this thing they called mediumship, and maybe I could help others with it. That November day, I realized the potential, especially for other bereaved parents such as myself. If I had to say what was the most important thing I wanted to know was that J.T. was okay. The second thing was that he knew I loved him and missed him so terribly. That was it. In that moment when I was receiving a message from another child who passed (with the help of my mentor) I saw very clearly what I needed to do. First, I needed to let this mom know her son was okay. Then I needed to get more messages from other children and get those messages to their parents. It seemed so clear to me and so necessary. I did not stop to think about what the parents' reactions would be.

The child's name was Zane. I knew his mother from the online grieving moms support group. I was so excited to give her the message, I posted all over the place to have her give me a call, to email me or something! I had to talk with her. Sandra, Zane's mom, emailed me with her telephone number. I remember going into my bathroom to talk with her because my kids were being very noisy outside my room. As other moms will attest, sometimes the bathroom is the only private room in the house. I knew I must have sounded crazed, but I wanted so much to have Sandra feel what I felt when I heard through Michelle that J.T. was fine. It was my very first reading, and I am sure I was not clear, but I hoped it would be enough so Sandra would have some peace that Zane is as close to her as J.T. is to me. I felt successful when I got off the phone and was energized to get more messages!

Opening up to the other side and allowing them to run the show did lead to some very terrifying experiences. I did not know how to control who was coming to me. My belief system was challenged further and I had to learn about my own power, and the Infinite power of my helpers on the other side. It is very important that we understand we do have full control over who comes to us as we are opening up. This was not something that was emphasized in my training, however I certainly emphasize it with my students. The reason I find people choose to not connect with their children is fear. Breaking through the fear of how this communication works and our part in this is critical to success.

I have to write about the one very scary and dark spirit who came to me one night. I do not want this to be the one thing you remember about this book, but understanding why it happened and how to prevent it from happening is an essential piece of this training. You do not have to learn as I did. You can learn from my mistakes.

My mentor believed if you stay on the high side of things, you will not encounter the low side. This may have been true for her but it was not true for me. The reason it was not true was because I had to interact with the low side since part of my job is to help them. At the time, I wanted no such thing in my awareness, and truly felt if I just ignored that whole aspect of things, I would be alright.

I was trying to connect with a young spirit named Sarah that November evening. I was such a newbie at connecting. I felt someone was close to me, so I asked, "Is this Sarah?" The response was a low male voice who said, "No. I am Ed." I could tell by his tone and energy he certainly was not Sarah. I could feel all the muscles in my stomach tighten. I got very scared and told him to go away. He did not go away. In fact, he ramped up his energy and tried to overpower me. It felt as if my insides were being torn into pieces.

I called my mentor immediately. No answer. I called repeatedly for hours. No answer. My dear friend, Monika, talked with me on the phone for hours. We were both so new at this. We tried different methods, rituals, incantations to get rid of Ed. He was having none of it.

I got so mad at J.T. for allowing this to happen. I thought he could protect me! I didn't realize my fears trumped everything.

The following morning at about 7 a.m. my mentor finally answered her phone. In tears, I told her what happened and how I was afraid to even leave my room for fear the energy would attach himself to my children. She checked in on the energy and then said, "OK. You should feel better now." I could still feel a cool breeze around me and was still in a panicked state. She said, "OK, how do you feel now?" The breeze felt softer. It was still cold, but much softer. As soon as I could catch my breath, I asked her, "What did you do? I have been trying all night!" She explained she felt into the energy and it was a very low energy, so she asked the angels to remove it. Poof! It was gone. At that moment, I became a believer in angels. Before this moment, I would have to say I wanted to believe in them, but had no direct experience to back it up. I asked her about the cool breeze around me. She told me it was the angels surrounding me and protecting me. She also set Archangel Ariel to be with me at all times. She told me to call to her whenever I felt scared, and she would let me know she was there. It must have been one hundred times each day for the following month I would call out to Arial. "Are you there?" I would ask. "Yes, I am here," I would hear in my head.

The biggest lesson I learned that night is that our helpers cannot help us if we do not believe they can. I included Michael in my meditations and automatic writing from that day on. He and I became very well acquainted. I believe wholeheartedly that I have a protector with me at all times. I call on Michael when I am in situations which unnerve me or if I feel threatened. He is always there and lets me know of his presence in so many ways.

What I learned from this experience:

I had to be comfortable with these low energies because I was going to help them move on their way and cross into the light.

I am the boss! Ed got the better of me because I did not believe in my own power. I believed he had all the power because I could not see him. The truth is I am the boss and what I say, goes!

If for some reason, I do not feel powerful, I have Michael protecting me. I call him the Cosmic Bouncer because he will "bodily" remove these energies. I can instantly feel them leave when I ask for Michael's help.

Not everyone will have this kind of experience because not everyone is supposed to have interactions with these energies! Do not let the fear of this stop you from connecting with your child!

I learned ghosts are real, but they really are only people without bodies. Many are just confused and need some help. There are some Eds out there. I work with them because I know I can help them. I am no longer afraid of them.

I understand now the purpose of that terrifying night was to truly experience it so I could include training for this in my program instead of taking the tact my mentor took. I understand the fears which hold people from connecting to the other side, and I have direct experience in successfully moving those energies out of my life. This does not mean you will have the same situation…in fact you will not! I will teach you how to call on Michael and feel that power.

The Kids Keep Coming

I learned so much in those next months. I learned that I opened myself up for randomness and frustration by allowing anyone and everyone to contact me. I learned it was acceptable to have boundaries and to set my "work" hours with spirits I couldn't see. I learned I was the boss, and they would just have to wait until I was ready for their message as opposed to waking me up in the middle of the night. I also learned I had to make time for them even if I was tired and afraid of my gift. It was the only way to get better at hearing the messages. I got so frustrated by my lack of clarity, I almost turned away from connecting. Then I would remember my boy and how hard he worked to get me here. I couldn't let him down. As frustrating and heartbreaking it was to do this work, I had to do it—for him, if nothing else.

Setting boundaries deserves some defining. I was so excited to have these children on the other side coming to me to give messages to their parents! At the same time, I was still very green and unsure I was hearing the message clearly. I had to repeat my boundaries over and over— "I am not working now. I am changing my baby's diaper. You need to come back when I am working." These kids were so eager to give the messages to me, and I was so new at setting boundaries, it felt so frustrating to have to continually reinforce my limits.

Again, I learned it was me. I still did not believe in my power. I still thought if I was given this gift, I should be available 24/7! That Catholic guilt again! My family needed me, too, though. My children had experienced this horrific event not even a year prior and I needed to be available for them. Those children would just have to understand.

Eventually, they did, and I have not had to reinforce this for years. I would go through phases where I was just so tired of trying to connect because it was "hard." Connecting, I found, was not hard. Removing my own blocks to connecting and my own ideas of how it should be was what made it "hard." During those times when I was not connecting regularly were the times when the children would interrupt my daily life and not wait until I was "working." I can't blame them. I was not taking the time to work so how else would they get the messages to me?

One March morning in 2008 I was doing my automatic writing and felt the presence of a girl with me. Automatic writing is sitting down and just typing what I hear. I will have an exercise for you later in this book so you can practice automatic writing if you choose. I asked for a name and she said Angel. I asked her, "Are you an angel or is your name

Angel?" She was very clear. Her name was Angel. A few days before, I heard from my husband there were two children killed in a car accident and the girl's name was Angel. I asked her if she was the girl in the accident. She said yes. I asked her if I knew her mom. She said no. This is where my job gets complicated. I was working very hard at getting messages from kids whose moms I knew. I was not very successful at getting messages to moms I did not know. I also was not comfortable enough with my gift to randomly call someone and tell them I had a visit with their dead daughter and here is what she said!

I took a little of the message and then I told Angel she needed to do some work for me. She needed to get her mother to cross my path. If she could do that, I would do my part and get the message to her mom. I did my part and sent her mother a letter I have which I send to any bereaved parent I encounter. I included the online support group information and my information if they wanted to contact me.

Less than a month later, I see a welcome email on my support group for this mom! Wow, I thought! Angel did her job. She got her mother to join the group and therefore, our paths crossed. I told Angel, "Good work!" and sent a personal message to the mom. I met with that mom and was able to give the messages from her children. What she does with those messages is up to her. I cannot have attachment to it and I was not there to prove myself. I was there to help these children let their mom know they were fine and very close by. This was an important lesson for me because not all people will believe what you say. It is not up to me to prove myself. It is my job to only give the message.

I Can See?

To this point, I relied mainly on my hearing to receive messages. There are four primary senses we use to receive information from the other side. Usually one is easier and stronger than the other and is called the "dominant clair." Clairaudience, or clear hearing, was my dominant clair. I could also feel, which is clairsentience. The other clairs are clairvoyance, clear seeing, and claircognizance, clear knowing. I attended a group psychic class twice a month as well as my one on one session with my mentor and was always so jealous of those who could "see." We think of psychics and mediums as being able to see the dead. I honestly thought I would not be a good medium until I could see them. Looking back I so appreciate having my hearing and realize it is a great way to receive information from the other side, but at the time I only focused on what I didn't have.

I remember clearly in one of the group practices we were working on the clairs and I said to the group, "I can't see." It was brought to my attention, of course I could not see because that is what I believed! From that moment forward, I said, "I am working on my seeing."

It was just about a week later when I *saw* my desires come to fruition! It was March 10, 2008. I was not even six months into my psychic training, but was advancing very fast and the information was coming so much more clearly.

I was sitting changing my four year old's diaper and got a zing that someone was there. This particular zing was right under my bra line on my left side, as if someone was poking me there. I grunted, thinking to myself "Can I please change this diaper without getting interrupted?" The response was a stronger zing to my side. Regardless of my desire to ignore the "call," the zinger would not stop! I realized this was not one of my guides letting me know he was there. I asked who it was. "Ben." "Oh, OK. Let me finish with my son and I will talk to you."

Ben is the son of a new friend of mine I met through the online support group. Ben's mother was having a very tough time with the impending one year anniversary of her son's death.

Before I even called her, I asked him if I could wait until the morning, or just email her. It was after 11 p.m. where she lived and I thought I'd be intruding. He said, "No, I want to talk to my mom tonight." I knew it was important to him, which meant it was also important to my friend. I checked in with my guide and asked him to check with hers to see if it was alright. He came back, "Yes, call."

I called, hoping I did not wake her up. I told her Ben was there. He really wanted his mom to know that he was there for his younger brother's birthday over the weekend. Earlier in the day, my friend said she could not feel him there. He was very concerned about this and wanted her to know that he was by her side. Then Ben gave me this feeling in my throat and chest. I was trying to figure out what it was. I asked my friend if she smoked. She said she did. Oh, that's why I feel like I just smoked a pack of cigarettes! I also felt a tightening in my chest, which I knew was her holding onto her grief and not letting it go. Ben was telling her that she needs to unbury herself so she can feel him again. I also felt a tightening in my stomach, which is where we hold our power, or feel out of control. I said to her, "You also feel out of control and are trying to control everything around you." She admitted to being a control freak. So I asked Ben to help his mom pull some of this helplessness out of her power center so she can deal with it. He showed me a scene where she was walking around a lake listening to music. My friend said she used to love to walk and listen to music; she doesn't anymore. Ben made it clear that was her ticket to freedom.

At one point, she said to Ben, "Tell Pop and Mom hello." I instantly got the picture of her dad in my head – round face, a little overweight, balding, glasses. She confirmed that was her dad. I got a major zing and said, "Hello Pop! What would you like to tell your daughter?" He said, "Ben is fine; he's with me. He's doing his work. We are OK. Don't worry about us. You need to do your work." It was so clear, like he was standing in my bedroom talking with me. I asked Pop what he was doing. He showed me his garden and how he was watering it. My friend confirmed he loved his garden. I told her he is also showing me he is drinking a cup of coffee, with cream in it. She said "Yes, he loved his coffee with cream." She asked if there were any slugs in his garden. He said, "No, we don't have any pests." He did show me a bunny in the garden. My friend confirmed her dad and mom used to raise rabbits!

We started talking about my friend's childhood. I got the image of her mother in my head—a very closed woman, cold, pursed lips, had a rough life and it was very hard on her. He also gave me the impression he was very strict. She verified all the impressions I was receiving. Then a very important message came through. "You have been given this opportunity so you do not become like that. You can be compassionate and caring," was the message from her dad. She agreed she has been looking in the mirror and feeling more and more like her mother. This is big, her dad said. She really needed to get this. She needs to do her work and uncover who she really is to find that happiness again.

She asked Pop if he forgave her for making the decision she did about letting him die. I started feeling pains in my stomach and became very nauseous. I knew it was cancer or chemotherapy. I can usually sense in my body when someone has passed from cancer because I feel the chemotherapy in my own body. She verified the treatments made him very ill. He thanked her for letting him go. He said it was his time and he was grateful to go. He was miserable being stuck in that body. He also said she made the right choice. My friend agreed. Pop was very thankful to have been freed.

Pop told her if she ever needed him to call and he would be there. I heard the Carole King song playing in my head. I assured her that all she had to do was call, and they both would be there.

We thanked Ben and Pop, and they thanked us. It was an amazing experience.

Getting off the telephone that night, I realized I could see! Both Ben and Pop showed me pictures in my head which were validated by my friend. I really could see! The information was so clear. I did not know it at the time, but so much of the clarity of the messages has to do with the spirit with whom I am communicating. I did not know this at the time and took full responsibility for any errors I made in interpreting messages. It was much later when I realized there are good communicators in spirit, and not so good communicators in spirit! I am very grateful Ben and Pop are good communicators!

CHAPTER SIX:
Still Grieving

J.T. was pushing me hard to learn as quickly as I could. It felt so overwhelming at times, but I wanted it so badly I would do anything to keep learning. I accomplished more than I believed possible in such a short period of time. All the while, J.T.'s antics kept me laughing instead of crying, for the most part. We were approaching the anniversary of his "death." I missed him so much and even while I was entrenched in learning this new life as a medium, I still had to grieve the loss of my little boy. It felt at times I was caught between the worlds – that world of grief and loss, anger and hurt, and the world where J.T. was, where everything was not just alright, but nirvana. I would get glimpses of his world in my meditations and daily life. There would be a flash here and a flash there. J.T. did not let a day go by without some sign or communication of some sort. I felt so blessed to be where I was. Where was I, though? Who was I?

Grief by itself creates an identity crisis. Am I still his mother? How many children do I have? How do I go from a mother of three to a mother of two? The answers were very clear from J.T. "Of course you are still my mother! You have three children...I am still here, Mom! More than you know!" Being very involved in the online bereaved mothers group, I received a daily dose of reality of who I was. I was a mom who had lost a child. There was a huge difference, though, between so many on that group and me. I had connection with my son. I knew where he was. I knew he was safe, and although I missed him so terribly, I could call to him and there he was! Each day the connection would be clearer and I would be able to spend more time talking with him. I looked so forward to my meditation time so I could connect with him! I was learning so much about where he was and what he was doing.

Sometimes the information I would receive caught me off guard. It would take a few days to process it, and millions of questions later, I would be satisfied with my understanding of whatever concept he was trying to teach me. Many new guides came in during that time who taught me different aspects of my abilities and how things worked on the other side.

One of my comrades through this craziness was a woman named Monica. We met through COVA, the online school I used for J.T. and then Lacey in the fall of 2007. One morning I opened my email to see a message from the one of the COVA teachers. She asked us to keep one of our COVA families in our prayers because the family's five year old son drowned. My heart ached so badly for them. Once you have personal experience with the loss of a child, any other children or families you hear about become like your own. You know the journey that family must endure and you know you cannot do anything to alter this journey, other than offer a hand so you can walk beside them.

I felt I had to reach out to this family, so I sent the mom an email telling her about J.T. and that I would be here for her. We began exchanging emails. She knew, just as I, there was a reason for her son's passing, and she was going to find it. I offered some of what worked for me. We finally spoke on the phone one day and I told her to listen – to get quiet and listen. She started to cry. She heard her beautiful son, Nik, say, "I love you, Mommy." From that moment forward, we would call each other when one of us would get new information from our sons. She was the only one on the planet who understood where I was and I was the only one who understood where she was. Her hearing was so clear. We used each other for validation when new information would come in. So many of the messages I was receiving were just crazy! I would call her up to find she got the same information! Our boys were certainly working together!

The day we met in person was just amazing. It felt like I had known Monica for lifetimes. We embraced and laughed and cried, all at the same time. Those who have experienced huge loss understand you can have all the gamut of emotions in the same moment. It sure is enough to make you think you are going insane! In that moment, all was sane for us, and everything we had experienced with the deaths of our children felt like it had purpose.

Monica and I are still very close. Our boys make sure we do not go for too long without talking. I am still so very grateful she came into my life. As much as we do not want to have anyone else with us in this wilderness, it sure is nice to have the company!

Life As Usual

As the rest of the world moves through their days, those who have lost a child can no longer see the road in front of them. There are many analogies I could use. We wake each day in a dust storm unable to see what is directly in front of us. We can hardly move as our legs feel waist high in mud. Our minds are so foggy, even we don't remember what we just said.

When the six month mark hits, we realize the world has moved forward but we are still in the same spot as when we heard our child was dead. I remember hitting that six month angelversary and feeling so lost. Reality begins to settle in that this isn't the nightmare from which we hoped we would awaken. This is real.

More time passes by and we hit those holidays. I was so grateful for those friends who stuck by my side. The first holiday season without J.T. was horrible. Every Christmas carol, every ornament, every wrapped present was a reminder there was still a big gaping hole in my family and in my heart, and there wasn't anything I could do to fill it. I resorted to buying my children more presents than they had ever seen. It was the only way I could think of to make up for their brother not being here. I know other families who chose to not celebrate at all. I thought about it, but I knew I had to do what I could for these kids. It wasn't their fault their brother died.

I tried to be the cheerleader on the support groups. Sometimes it worked; other times it did not. I learned we all had to be where we were, whether that meant the pits of grief or on the edge of it. I did my best to honor where others were and meet them there to try to help. I knew one of the things I would do with this is walk beside those newly bereaved parents and tell them what I learned and how I managed to survive those months.

My gifts were coming in very quickly, and when I could, I shared what I was learning from J.T. For so many, this was very threatening to their belief system. I wanted to meet them where they were, but I wasn't there anymore. I had more answers now than I ever dreamed and I understood why J.T. had to leave. How do you translate this to someone who does not believe our children can talk to us?

Many parents do believe our children can bring us signs, but it seems to be more from God than from their child. After all, to them, God was the one who took their child away. Trying to explain our children had choice in their leaving did not bode well with many of the moms on the support groups. I did my best to honor their beliefs, but at the same time honor their children. J.T. would remind me I didn't have to "save" everyone. Using their vernacular, I would say I wanted to "witness" to as many as possible that their child is still very much alive! It was a hard line to walk and I am sure I fell on one side or the other at times as I got my bearings on how to do this work.

The Anniversary

Our bodies remember trauma. They remember the situation. They remember the time of day. They remember the season of the year. J.T. left in the spring. We buried him just a few days before Easter Sunday. I could feel my anxiety levels get higher and higher as March 2008 approached. It felt like I was gearing up for something horrible to happen. I was anxious all the time, looking behind me and in front of me, waiting for something to jump out at me. I had never experienced a panic attack until J.T. left. I had heard about them but they were not in my reality. All common sense and logic goes out the window when you have buried a child. Fear, anxiety and this feeling of impending doom overwhelm your senses and paralyze you. Never in my life had I felt anything like this. I had no control over when it would happen, or where. Would I be driving on the freeway? Would I be in the middle of my children's school?

Who knew? I just prayed for mercy and for a quick passing of the attack. Sometimes they would hit me in the morning when I would look out my kitchen window. The way the sun was hitting the house threw me back into that place a year prior. The sun would come into the kitchen window at a certain angle in the spring. That dread would hit me and I would almost fall to my knees as the pain of the grief came flooding back. I did not consciously remember the sun coming into the window at that angle, but my body did. I remember saying to myself, how does it know?

I spent most of March 2008 in this state of panic. Mixed in were memories of the last time J.T. did this, or the last time he did that. It was so excruciating. For the entire year, you think of all the firsts you must endure without your child there with you. That last month for me was all the lasts I had with him— the last time he went rollerskating, the last time we went to LEGO® Club, or the last outing we had with his friends at the Loveland Children's Day earlier that month.

I struggled with what I knew from my psychic training and the human feelings I had being a mother who so desperately missed her boy. I knew I needed to do something to honor him, so I wrote a memorial for our local paper and put his picture with it. It ran on March 30, 2008. Here is what it said:

Remembering J.T.:   The Journey of a Year

It is every mother's fear that her child will be forgotten. One year ago today, our precious seven year old son passed away. These past twelve months, we have learned so much about life, and death, and everything in between. In memory of my son, J.T., I wanted to share some of what I have learned with you.

Wishes. That dreadful day last year, March 30, 2007, is one our family wishes we could forget. We wish we could turn back the hands of time and have our son still with us. We wish his younger sister and brother wouldn't have to learn about the finality and frailty of the human body at such young ages.

Mostly, we wish this would never have to happen to anyone else on the planet. But it does. I've learned......To make those wishes count today. Don't wait until tomorrow to take your children to the park, or to the movies, or just to the basement to play games together. You might not get a tomorrow. We didn't. We hope you never have to say, "I wish...."

Camaraderie. We are so grateful to those who rallied around us, supported us, and held us in the moments of our darkest days and nights. If you would have given me a list on March 29th of those who would still be by my side one year later, I would have laughed heartily! It is not until you experience a loss as great as ours, that you experience a love as great as our friends. We are more than blessed to have the most caring, funny, wonderful friends. I've learned...What FRIEND means. What kind of friend are you? Would you stay by a friend's side even if it meant you must witness incredible pain and suffering? Or would you be one of the "well-meaners" who stand in the background and hope they "get over it quickly". I know now after what I have experienced I am a friend who would be there no matter how much pain I had to see or feel. I don't know if I could say that about myself prior to March, 30, 2007.

Laughter. Anyone who knew my J.T. can still hear him laughing, even a year after his death. He had this belly laugh that would make anyone turn to see what was so hysterical! He would laugh at stupid jokes, funny cartoons (he loved Tom and Jerry), playing tricks on his brother and sister, and sometimes his mom and dad! If you ask someone the one thing they would remember about J.T., it would either be his "never give up" attitude, or his laughter. It's been hard for me to laugh over this past year. I know he wants me to laugh, but doing it has been hard. And then when I did laugh, I felt guilty, like laughing was disrespectful to my son. I know now this is not true, but any grieving parent will tell you, it's hard to laugh without guilt. I've learned….laughter is an essential part of life. Do you laugh? Really laugh? Maybe it's time to break out those "Three Stooges" DVDs, or one of my favorites, "Airplane." Try not laughing at that!

Never give up. I mentioned the two things people remember most about J.T., and "never giving up" was one of them. I've never had as much determination as that young seven year old. He would keep at something, regardless of what it was, until he got it right. One of the last events we attended was at the roller rink earlier in March 2007. It was his first time on roller skates. Do you think he gave up after the first few falls on his behind? Absolutely not. He kept going and kept going and kept going. I cannot say he "mastered" roller skating after one trip, but he worked so hard and improved dramatically by the end of the day. He used the same philosophy in Karate. He loved Karate and worked so hard. In honor of his tenacity, the Karate school created a special award in his name, the "J.T. Baptista Never Give Up" award. We are so proud of our son and so thankful to Northern Colorado Karate for memorializing our son with this award, as well as for their friendship, support and help over this year. I've learned…if a seven year old can give his all to everything, so can I.

Love is all there is. With everything else gone, buried in the ground, what I have left of my J.T. is this amazing love of mother and son. Time can never take that from me. I might have to donate his clothes, give his toys to his siblings, and do my best to preserve his artwork from school and the pictures in his Batman costumes. But I will never ever have to worry about his fading love for me or mine for him. We come into this world with nothing, and we leave with nothing. You hear it over and over again. "You can't take it with you." There's not much for a seven year old to take, quite frankly. And even if there was, would it matter? What matters is how much we love him. After all, if we didn't love him so very much, this sharp, never-ending pain of missing him so much would not be a part of our daily existence. It might sound strange to say, but I will take this pain, because it means I love someone THAT much. I love someone with all my heart and soul, and I will never recover from having to bury him that spring day in 2007. But the love we have can never be buried, will never die, unless we let it. I've learned…Life is nothing without love.

Our journey is far from over. Fifty-two weeks is not very long when you face so many years without seeing a loved one. But I do have more understanding about life, and death, and everything in between, thanks to our wonderful, beautiful son, J.T. We love you, buddy, and we always will.

The Process

I want to address the grief process at this point. Most bereaved parents will tell you, when you hit the one year mark, the support of your family and friends fades significantly. All they want for you is the best. They want you to return to the person you were before your child died. This is not possible. You cannot will it into existence, no matter how hard you try to alter your current reality. I have had many moms tell me their families and friends have told them to stop talking about their children and just get on with their lives.

No matter what the motivation is to say this to a bereaved parent, it is wrong. I got very tired of being judged for my grief process and I know the majority who are reading this book probably feel the same. Between learning more about grief, my own process and then including the training I was receiving, I learned to not judge others for their judgments of me.

It would have been easy enough to say, "Well #$%# YOU! Get the hell out of my life!" Just as I had caught myself that day of my son's viewing when the woman told me the cough syrup probably killed my son, I did my best to understand the person's point of view. Many times, I did walk away because I realized this person did not understand me and it was better to leave than to engage.

They say grief rewrites your address book. This is very true, especially after the one year mark. I had many people leave my life in that year, but also many people came in. I learned to let go of those who could not handle my grief or my new career because I knew there would be someone so very special who wanted to be a part of my life and accepted me for who I was.

Regardless of what you are told about grief, the stages of grief, the faces of grief, you must do it your own way. I need to add, though, avoidance of grief only creates more grief. The only way to get to the other side of it is through it. Believe me; I have tried all the other ways! The other side of grief to me means the return of joy in my life. I struggled with this concept, though. Wasn't having joy and happiness return to my life a dishonoring of my son? Shouldn't I be miserable for the rest of my life to honor that life which was taken so young? I remember feeling so guilty when I would laugh. J.T. told me NO! He said, "You honor me by laughing again, by smiling, by bringing others joy. You honor me by telling others about me and telling them they can talk to their kids, too. You honor me by taking this hole in your heart and planting the seeds so someday, the flowers will fill the hole." My dear friend, Kari Koppes, has this beautiful sculpture of a woman with a hole in her heart, but in that hole are just a few flowers which fill the once empty space. Kari lost her husband, Cubby, in 1998. She was one of those dear souls who would come over every night with a vodka tonic in hand and just talk. She and I have ridden those grief waves together. I am so very grateful for her. As hard as those waves tried to crush us, we would roll on the shore, drinks still in hand, laughing at the thought of Cubby and J.T. watching us crack morbid jokes about death and urns and caskets. We would always say, "Well, we could cry or we could laugh. We are choosing to laugh."

The Little Ones

My children were five and three when their brother left. Death is so hard on children. Much of this can be avoided by telling them the truth about it. Nothing was harder than coming home that morning on March 30, 2007, to tell my two little ones they would not be seeing their brother again. During those first months, the books poured in about how to talk to children about death and what to say, what not to say. Much of the information just didn't feel right. I did my best to let them cry and scream. I watched for signs of acting out, anger and fear. I reminded them many times J.T. is still with us, we just can't see him.

I searched for a therapist for them who understood sibling grief. No one had this "specialty" or experience. I knew having no therapist was better than one who couldn't relate, so we muddled through that first year as best we could.

As I was learning to hear J.T., I began teaching my children how to hear him, see him and feel him. I would take them to the cemetery to "visit" their brother as often as I thought it was healthy for them. Anthony would take off and run around looking at all the markers. He and Lacey would play in the snow as I sat on a blanket or chair next to J.T.'s grave. It was my way of keeping my kids together. In the spring, we would laugh at the dragonflies trying to land on both Lacey and Anthony, and joke it was J.T.'s way of playing with them.

I remember one day very distinctly. Lacey was sitting on my lap as I was on my blanket next to J.T. She knew I was crying a bit. I asked, "You know I love you, Lacey. Don't you?" Very plainly, she said, "No I don't." I asked her why. She said, "Because you don't cry over me. You just cry over J.T." I realized my grief was impacting my children. From that moment on, I made sure I was alone when I had my grief fits. Yes, I did still cry in front of my children, but not like I had.

There's a fine line between showing them too much and not showing them enough.

Eventually, I found a good therapist for them in Boulder. The point is you do the best you can with what you can, and that's that. There's no one answer, and the answer changes day to day anyway.

Honor your grief and honor your children's grief – whatever that means to you.

CHAPTER SEVEN
The Second Year

The experts say the second year is harder than the first when you have lost a child. I remember bracing myself as that one year mark passed. I also remember others in my support group finding the grief pit much harder to navigate in their second year. I wondered what was wrong with me because the second year was not harder. It was almost a relief that the year had passed and it felt more like I could begin to rebuild now that I passed the anniversary of J.T.'s "death." I had gone through all the firsts without him (including appendicitis on Mother's Day weekend and a horrible virus attacking Anthony), and I had gone through all the memories of the lasts of everything in that last month. I can say I was ready for a new beginning. I tried to share this with my other bereaved moms, but for so many, they just could not relate to where I was in my grief process.

My training was progressing rapidly and my connection with J.T. was clearer every day. I started doing practice readings on my friends and found I was very accurate, when I would get out of my own way. I was excited to start helping other moms and dads who so missed their children. I did what I was told by my mentor and my guides. I found if I listened and followed their directions, life became so much easier!

My main communications with my guides was through automatic writing. This is a practice I recommend to all of my students whose dominant clair is clairaudience, or clear hearing. A dominant clair is the sixth sense which comes the easiest. For me, it was hearing, so my training focused on this clair. I began with thirty minutes of meditation. The meditation raised my awareness and allowed clearer communication. Then I sat at the computer and brought up a blank word processing document. I set my intention which is saying aloud the name of the person with whom I wanted to communicate, and then said my prayer of protection. I closed my eyes and asked for the energy to come close to me so I could hear. I would ask, "Who is here with me?" and type the answer I heard. Usually, I would ask for a high guide or an expert in the subject about which I was learning at the time. I received so much information in advance of it actually happening, which validated my experience and certainly pushed me to keep asking those crazy questions.

I helped organize an apprentice psychic fair in June 2008. It was for the students in the psychic program of which I was a part. I was terrified to give readings to the public, but I had worked so hard getting it all together and I knew the other students were counting on me just as much as I was counting on them to get us through one of the more frightening days of our psychic lives. I did not realize the impact my words would have on those who sat across from me receiving that reading. Who could imagine the peace and healing from simple words like, "He is OK" or "She is so happy now and out of pain"?

I was reminded of how much it matters what I do at a Reiki class I taught just a couple of weeks ago. One of the attendees was a lady who went to that psychic fair almost four years ago. She received one of the flyers we canvassed around town. Her brother was missing. She sat down at my table and asked me if I could help her find her brother. Checking in, I knew he was not alive. I called my mentor over and between the two of us, we told her what happened to her brother. All these years later, she told me it was exactly as we had told her. The people responsible for her brother's death were caught about a year ago. That day she entered that fair with a bunch of very unsure psychic and mediums, she left with answers and a sense of relief. We could not bring her brother back, but we could tell her how he comes to visit and the ways he leaves little presents for her to find. I am in awe of the accuracy of the information we receive from Spirit. I get a daily dose of this amazing connection, and I am still surprised at the miracles I see every day.

At the time, I was still feeling green, but knew I was supported more than I could ever imagine. In October 2008, I was directed to have my first intuitive workshop. This direction was from my guides and not necessarily from my mentor. She encouraged me to a certain extent, but I felt I needed to be cautious about stepping on her toes. I did worship her, which was my own fault. I soon learned when one is put upon a pedestal, it is a set up for a major fall.

Honestly, I did not feel I was ready to do this group training. I had only been in training for a year and thought it was like any other trade – you needed to put in your dues prior to becoming the "expert." My guides thought very differently, however. They wanted me to start training others right away. I would have conversations with J.T. about it. He reminded me I did not have to know everything! The guides would fill in where they needed and all I had to do was listen. Again, when I listened, it was so clear!

November 2008 was the turning point for me. The Psychic Mentoring group of which I was a part had become my family. I looked forward to being with them twice each month and exploring my new abilities, learning more about myself, and feeling part of this intimate group. I was mortified after the November group class when my mentor misinterpreted something I did, which forced me leave the group. I asked J.T. what happened and, more importantly, what was I supposed to do now? I felt lost and so unprepared for the road ahead. My guides had shown me all of these things I was supposed to do – readings, individual training, and workshops! I was distraught and felt like I would have to give up entirely! Certainly, I was not ready to be on my own yet. In my heart, I knew I wasn't really on my own. We are never "on our own." We all have this amazing support system on which we can call day or night. They are always there for guidance and comfort. My dear friend, Monica, helped me get some answers from my guides. Because of my emotional state, I thought I surely had misheard what they said. She confirmed I needed to leave that group because I would always feel I needed to stay a step behind my mentor. The situation was created so I would have no choice but to go out on my own. The guides knew I would not rock the boat or "show up" my mentor, and the truth was, I needed to soar. Through Monica, they reminded me they would tell me what I needed to do and train me from that point forward. I came to the realization that I could not move forward if I stayed in the group, and the places I needed to go and the people I needed to assist far outweighed my necessity for a human teacher.

I continued to learn from my guides and quickly realized how much faster I could move without the group holding me back. I guess my guides knew what they were doing after all! I was a faithful, obedient student, and I was about to learn how much that would pay off, not only for me but for many others seeking guidance and training.

The Call To Teach

A very special lady and her family came to that apprentice psychic fair I organized that June. Her name was Michelle Eller. Her dear friend's son passed about a year prior and she was looking to connect with him. I did not know at the time she saw my name and knew I would have the answer for her. She came and sat right down, and we connected with Gage, her friend's son.

Michelle also attended that first intuitive workshop I had. She told me I needed to start mentoring others. I looked at her like she was crazy! Me? Teach others how to connect? You are nuts, I would tell her! At the same time she was nudging me, my guides told me it was time. Time for what? "Time to teach," they answered! I was introduced to my new teaching team. It was a group of five teachers from the other side. They would instruct me on what I needed to do with each student. As long as I followed their direction, the training would be successful!

I had my first student, Jaime Parrott, begin in January 2009, just a couple of months before J.T.'s second angelversary. Jaime was Michelle's sister. I learned later Jaime saw J.T.'s picture in the paper when we printed his obituary. Who knew two years later, that precious little boy would lead her to me?

I had many conversations with my teaching team prior to starting this new adventure. They worked so diligently with me. I trusted them implicitly. There were many times when I had no idea where they were taking me. I felt blind, but guided. J.T.

was there by my side helping me adjust to my new instructions and new life. I would follow him anywhere! My guides knew I would not have come this far without my son, and we were both so happy to be working together.

I could not believe how easily the information flowed for Jaime. We called in her guides and my teaching guides and we were off and running! They knew exactly what her strengths were and her weaknesses. We honed her strengths and developed her less than strong aspects. Each month we would meet and work on something different for her. She was soaking it up and doing the homework the guides gave her. As long as I listened and focused on what the guides were saying and not what I was thinking, it flowed so smoothly. Both Jaime and I were amazed at the results. We would pat each other on the backs at the end of the sessions – we both listened and received exactly what we needed. Jaime and I now travel together to conferences and conduct our own workshops. What a blessing she and her family have been to me!

Where Did Everyone Go?

During this time when I was learning so much about who I was, I also discovered so much about other people. I discovered during this time having a soul purpose outside the "acceptable" societal careers can be quite challenging, for both my intellect and my self esteem. I was on a whirlwind journey, attempting to find my why in the vastness of this mixed up world where up was down and down was up. Thanks to my boy and my determination, I was blessed to discover what I came to this planet to do, what I have been preparing many lives to do, and what my son on the other side was eagerly helping me do. In a nutshell, I could hear dead people.

This generally was not my opening line at a party when I first met someone, nor was it what I put on my business cards. Even after preparing many of my friends with the front questions – "What are your beliefs of the afterlife?" "Do you believe in angels?" and especially "Do you think they try to communicate with us?" – I found very few in my current life were able to hear my answers to these questions. Frankly, I think they believed I was in a previously undocumented stage of grief, and surely would require some sort of medication to bring me back to my reality. I already had the stigma of losing a child, which terrifies those already fearful souls to the core. When I would tell them my son still hangs out with me and is helping me with my life's purpose, they would get that "circus freak" look in their eyes and head for home.

At first, I took their rejection very personally. After all, I was still grieving and I could sure have used those phone calls they told me they would make, and those drop bys they promised after everyone else went back to their regular lives. Through it all, I kept telling myself that there was a reason they were leaving my life and it would all become clear. That's what the Universe does, if you let energy flow where it needs to flow and get out of the way. It clears the path.

Then something amazing happened. New souls came into my life – very courageous souls who were also forging this road, who were also being chastised and forgotten. It wasn't only me! I learned about the Law of Attraction and realized that when I was true to my purpose and honest with myself and others about my purpose, I would be aligned with those who have the ability, knowledge and willingness to help me! "Wow!" I thought. How cool is that?

What I now understand is the Universe was making way in my life for something so big and beautiful, that even I could not imagine it with my human mind. Those who had to "leave me behind" were in fact doing so out of necessity. I no longer had to feel uneasy around them. I didn't have to feel the need to explain anything anymore. They didn't have to wonder if I knew what a loon they thought I was. I was free.

I was still open and welcomed anyone into my life who wanted to be on this road with me. At the same time, I felt freed from the burden between being true to myself and appeasing those who were not able to support me on this new journey and who just wanted me to go back to the way I was. That was impossible, even if I wanted to do that, which I didn't.

It was not an overnight process, but each time I was able to say, "I am a psychic medium and I connect people to their loved ones on the other side…and by the way, my son is always by my side," I felt victory in being the person I came here to be. I also learned what a judging, critical person I was before J.T. left. Those judging me were a reflection of the old me buried with my son in March 2007. I knew I could not be around those who judged me any longer. It was a painful, but very necessary process I needed to go through to wean myself from them. I could not hold myself back, though, because I did not live up to their ideals.

Remember this through this process of learning to connect. Do not let others dictate how you do this or what it looks like. That is totally up to you.

CHAPTER EIGHT
The Doors Open

The dreaded two year mark had just passed. It was April 2009. I was still grieving my son, but had found a brand new world ahead of me and I knew it was going to get even crazier! J.T. would tease me with phrases like, "Just wait, Mom!" and "We have so many surprises for you!" I am sure it was his way of keeping me motivated and anticipating the future.

I had my careers in selling through direct marketing and life insurance companies, so my first inclination was to sell myself and my services. I knew this wasn't the way to get where I needed to go, and that I needed to be patient. Patience. When I was in my twenties, I would beg for patience. I told myself I would have patience when I was thirty. When I was in my thirties, I told myself I would have patience when I was forty. I am in my forties now…where is that patience?! The virtue of patience has been a lifelong lesson for me. Nonetheless, I was patient! I did not advertise my services and I followed the guidance from my guides and J.T., and I waited.

I saw many other mediums on stage connecting the audience with their loved ones on the other side, but the thought of being on stage terrified me. I was still wrestling with the "I'm a fake" demon and the "what if I am wrong?" doubts in my head. The last thing I would ever want to do is be onstage in the public eye to be criticized and ridiculed. This was not my idea of a good time.

I was invited to a reception for Rev. Michael Beckwith and his wife Rickie at a church in town. The following day, Rev. Beckwith was speaking at the Lincoln Center, the same venue where I saw John Holland one and a half years prior. I did not purchase a ticket to that event, though, for a reason I cannot recall, really. The Universe obviously wanted me to go anyway!

Earlier that week, a ticket landed in my lap from someone who had purchased it but could not go. I jumped on the chance, especially since I would be attending the reception the night before.

If you are not familiar with Rev. Michael Beckwith, he is an astounding spiritual speaker and teaches universal truth principles found in the New Thought-Ancient Wisdom tradition of spirituality. This means he helps people get in touch with their highest good.

That evening at the Lincoln Center, Rev. Beckwith led us in a meditation to discover our higher purpose. I watched him on that huge stage at the Lincoln Center, soaking up everything I could. I went into the meditation very easily and followed his words as I found myself in a different place. I take that back, it was the same place, but it was I who was on that huge stage looking out at all the people instead of Rev. Beckwith! I jolted out of the meditation. I was surprised, to put it mildly. I immediately asked my guides, "Am I supposed to be on stage doing my work?" "Well, yes, Sarina, you are." Stupefied, I wandered to my car after the lecture was over, partly curious, partly excited, very terrified! How in the world am I going to do this? The answer was clear, again, "You are not going to do this. We are going to do this." Good thing, I thought. I am certainly not ready for this one! "Do not worry," they replied. "You will be."

Who Ya Gonna Call?

If you recall, I had an encounter with a very nasty spirit named Ed in the beginning of my training. The mere thought of these low vibrations coming into my "sphere" still scared me. A friend of mine started doing some ghost hunting with a local paranormal group. Not my cup of tea, I told her! She called me one morning and asked if I would help her cross some of the spirits she had encountered the night before. This was a new concept to me. Crossing spirits into the light was not part of my awareness, and truthfully, I wasn't sure I wanted it to be. I really didn't even know what this meant. I did some research online about it, and I also knew we would be guided on what to do and how to do it. I knew I needed to get over my fear of that realm since my encounter with Ed, so I agreed.

We went to Roger's Grove Park in Longmont, Colorado, a notorious place for spirits to hang out, so to speak. We sat down where my friend had first encountered the spirits. It was not long before we knew we were not alone. I would have thought I was going crazy, making it all up in my head, but we both were hearing and feeling the same things.

We asked our guidance what we were supposed to do to get these spirits into the light. We did as we were told and could feel them go through us and into this circle of light we were creating for them. Honestly, if I wasn't an actual participant, I wouldn't have believed it was possible. I didn't believe in ghosts. I figured there was this really ugly place those really ugly people went when they died, but I wanted no part of it.

My guides had different ideas, though. I found later I had agreed to help these spirits get to where they needed to go. That day at Roger's Grove, I was just following orders. I knew enough to follow orders.

Stunned at what had just happened, we looked at each other with that "Did you just feel that, too?" look. We decided to go further down the path to see what else, or who else, we would find. As we walked, I felt an energy rush at me! It was a woman who was very angry. She was yelling at us, "Why did you do that? Now I am all alone!" Again, my friend and I received the same words. All I could feel was this anger, rage and then despair and sorrow. I knew these were not my emotions, and I knew these were not my words coming into my head. We followed our guides again and opened the light. Now what we saw was very different. We saw her friends come back to get her, and away they all went!

Driving home that night was very unnerving. Had I just opened Pandora's Box? Why was I even doing this? I asked J.T. for help to figure out this new world. What did we do at Roger's Grove? What does it mean to "open the light"? Do I have to do this, because I don't want to? Who were these spirits anyway?

Over the course of the next few months, I delved into the paranormal with great fervor. I understood about vibrational energies and how to keep my vibration high so I could connect to my helpers, so what was with these other lower energies? They felt so dense, and did not seem to have the same awareness as those who had "crossed over." Why?

What I learned was just one version of the story. I'm sure there are others just as valid. There are pieces that I am still learning; the Universe is so complex in many ways, and so simple in others.

What I was told by my guides was that when we leave our bodies, our energy is so close to the vibration as when we were in our bodies. This is why people see their loved ones so clearly when their loved ones first pass. It is so much easier for a spirit to manifest in those first days and weeks because they are so close to our vibrational level. Some people whose bodies die choose to stay at that vibrational level. They might fear damnation or a judging God, or hell. They see the light, but they turn away from it.

Honestly, this is not the majority. The majority do feel the love and peacefulness of heaven, or the other side, or whatever you call it, and have no hesitation. When I asked J.T. what he experienced, he said it was like the tubes at Chuck E Cheese. Leave it to a seven year old to have a play structure be his way to heaven!

I found that if I set my intention that my hands would open up a doorway to the other side, those who were ready to go would come from miles around and cross to the other side. It did not matter where I was, either. If someone needed help, they would find me and ask to cross! It was kind of a joke in our family when I would excuse myself to use the restroom when we were in public. My husband would ask me if I was really going to go, or did I just need to help someone cross?

I joined a paranormal group that welcomed psychics. Many groups are not "psychic friendly." My sole purpose for joining was to assist those spirits who wanted to cross. We would do the investigation and then open the light at the end of the night for all those who wanted to move on their way. Whatever their reasons or fears, I would talk to them and let them know what my son told me about where they were going. Sometimes, I would need to bring in one of their loved ones to help them cross, and sometimes J.T. would come to assist.

I learned part of my work was to help these souls continue on their journey and to demystify the idea of ghosts among the living. I started clearing these energies from houses and taught homeowners how to reclaim their space. I taught people how to connect with their guides so they could call on them to assist them here without the worry of calling on the "wrong" energy. This was so important to me because when I began my journey I was so clueless about energy and how everything worked on this planet and where J.T. was.

I also learned not all mediums need to deal in this realm. I know for some it is very scary, as it was for me in the beginning. I deal in this realm because I said I would in my contract. I know I am a powerful soul and these souls who have chosen to stay earthbound, as it is called, are only as powerful as we allow them to be. You do not need to deal with these spirits to connect. The next chapters will teach you how to connect with only those energies and people you wish to connect.

Ghost Week

The week before Halloween is known as Ghost Week at one of our radio stations here. I was listening to Scott and Sadie in the morning on Big Country 97.9FM on October 29, 2009 as I was driving my children to school. All week I had tried to call into their show to tell them about my paranormal experiences, but the lines were always busy! This day turned out to be a snow day for my kids, so I was driving them back home when I tried one more time to get through to the station. Lo and behold, Scott James answered the phone and asked, "Ghosts. Are they real or not?" I replied, "Yes, they are real!" He said, "How do you know?" I told him I was part of a paranormal group here in town and have had my share of personal experiences with these "ghosts." He said, "What are you doing right now?" and invited me to come to the station to talk with them and their listeners about my experiences!

I drove home to change, grabbed one of my fellow ghost hunters and head to the station.

We got to the station and were escorted up to the Big Country studio. We were introduced to Scott and Sadie and immediately Scott looks at my friend and says, "You are a medium, aren't you?" My friend told him both of us were mediums. The show switched from just talking about the paranormal to also talking about people's loved ones on the other side.

As I was sitting there talking with them, I could feel J.T. right beside me and boy, did he have a smile on his face! I thanked him in my head for providing this opportunity for us. His reply was "The best is yet to come!"

After the show, my friend and I put together a proposal for the station on having a regular psychic segment for their morning show. It took a few months to work out, but in February 2010, we had our Psychic Thursday segment! First it was every other month as we were splitting time with another medium. In June, it became our show, and in July, it became my show! Looking back, I know the guides were easing me into it. Had I been responsible for the show every month on my own right away, I would have felt so overwhelmed, and possibly quit altogether. Each step I was ready to take. I am still the resident psychic for Big Country 97.9FM and we do a show every year at Halloween time to connect listeners with their loved ones. I am so grateful for the friendships I have now with Scott James and Sadie Koehler. They are wonderful people and I would not have had the opportunity to meet them and get to know them if I hadn't made that random call that Thursday before Halloween as I drove my kids back home from school.

Look at Me—I'm On Stage!

There are no coincidences. The Universe, God, Source, whatever you call that Divine Energy knows exactly where we need to be and does everything possible to get us there – sometimes kicking and screaming, if necessary!

That February when I began the Psychic Thursday show, I was also being pushed to begin my "stage" work. This was more terrifying to me than anything else. I was still wrestling with the whole notion that I wasn't as good as I thought I was and, surely if I tried to connect an audience with their loved ones, I would be found out. I would be called a fake and be the joke of Loveland, Colorado.

A medium from out of town was doing an event at the church one of my friends attended, so we decided to go. Her name was Kimmie Rose Zapf and she was a friend of Donna Visocky who I knew from the psychic group. Donna owns BellaSpark Productions and is responsible for bringing so many spiritual and inspirational speakers to our area. She also has a child on the other side, Kristi, so Donna and I understand each other on a level most don't ever experience.

It hit me as I was watching Kimmie. She made connecting with loved ones and giving psychic messages to the audience look so easy! It became very real to me that I could do this. I could connect audiences to the other side. I could do what she does, and what John Holland does, and what Lisa Williams does. I can make a difference to those people out there begging for something from their loved one, something to let them know they are okay.

That evening I asked J.T. if I was ready. He told me I had been ready for a while, and then he laughed. I love his laugh. That beautiful belly laugh of his I miss so much hearing with my physical ears I can still hear with my "inner ears." I would need a venue, I told him. Somewhere I wouldn't have to pay to rent, but somewhere I felt comfortable enough to be in front of a large group of people. I rattled some ideas around in my head, but it wasn't clear enough yet.

Kimmie's event was a Friday night. Sunday, I went to my usual coffee house, The Coffee Tree, which is inside Anthology Book Company in downtown Loveland. I always see events advertised for Anthology. I walked around and asked my guides, "Is this it? Is this the place?" A resounding YES reverberated through my head! Great, I thought. Now what do I do? I knew one of the employees; Teresa was the daughter of Anthony's preschool teacher, Laura Martinez. Maybe she was working and I could run it past her what she thought of the idea. Instead, the owner, Stephanie Stauder, was at the counter. I introduced myself and told her my idea. She was thrilled! She told me she was working on an idea like this but did not know where to start. She also told me she usually was not in on Sundays, but this particular Sunday she decided to stop by. I thanked my guides, knowing they engineered the meeting for both of us. We decided on a date in March – March 27th. This was just three days before J.T.'s angelversary. I knew it was J.T.'s way of keeping me busy, looking forward rather than back to that point in time when he left me. What better model to connect people to their loved ones on the other side than a mom grieving her son. I know the pain, and I know how much it meant to find out my son was safe, happy and still very much alive.

Before I knew it, March 27th was here. I had no idea what I was doing, how it all worked, how I would receive information, or if anyone would show up! I had faith my son would not let me down or set me up for failure. I will never forget how scared I was. The seats were filling with people who came to see me "perform." I smiled as I usually do, very large and inviting. No one knew me. I did have my "posse" there – Jaime Parrott and Michelle Eller were my cheerleaders. Thank God they were there. I probably would have walked out if they weren't there to help me. Jaime was my scheduler, flyer distributor, sign up sheet monitor, and anything else she needed to do. I was so grateful to have her and Michelle there. It gave me the freedom to prepare for what I was about to do.

The clock kept ticking closer and closer to the event start time. My inner clock ticked louder and louder, screaming, "What are you doing?? You can't do this!!" I went into the bathroom to calm myself. I looked in the mirror. Seriously. What am I doing? I can't do this. I have no idea what I am doing. How am I going to connect with anyone? How does this all work? I can't do this. Whose idea was this in the first place? I was in full panic mode; my mind was racing, trying to find a way out! J.T. did what he does best. In an instant, all those thoughts left my mind. My mind's eye showed a dark screen. I heard in my head, "Speed. I am Speed." This was followed by the opening scene in the Disney Cars movie where all the cars were zooming past – Zoom! Zoom! Zoom! I bursted into laughter! Playing in my head was the scene where Lightening McQueen was in his trailer before the race psyching himself up to be the fastest car on the track! J.T. said, "Mom, you are psyching yourself out. This is so much easier than you think it is." I laughed for a while at myself, and at J.T. for picking the perfect remedy for my panic attack! He loves the Disney movie Cars, and we would watch that scene over and over. I thanked him and let him know I did trust him, and I would go out there and do what I do best – connect and follow instructions.

I left the bathroom with a smile on my face. I still had no idea what I was doing, but I knew this was the only way to figure it out, and I had help.

I introduced myself, pulling on all of the direct marketing experience I had speaking in front of groups. I told them a little about myself, and as I was talking, I could feel the room fill up with spirits. They started nudging me, telling me they wanted to talk to their loved ones, so could I please move the show along? I started chuckling at the conversations in my head and the conversation I was trying to have with those in the audience. I still did not know how this would work, other than what I had seen at other mediums' events.

I began the connecting part of the evening and felt a very strong male presence. I asked the energy what relation he was to his person in the audience. He told me he was Father. He started showing me very clear pictures. The first image I saw was him in these wild rainbow socks. I told the audience, "Someone's father is here and he is showing me he is in these crazy socks. They look like socks a clown would wear. Rainbow colors. Does anyone resonate with that?" Nothing. Silence. I started to panic just a bit. This was my first spirit through! If I don't get someone to acknowledge this guy, what are my chances to get anyone to acknowledge anything? I asked him for more. He showed me a different rainbow. This was a picture of a poofy rainbow with poofy white clouds at one end. Again, I asked, "Does this make any sense to anyone here?" Crickets. In my head I started to panic. I asked J.T., "What do I do?" He said, "Look around the room." I looked at the audience to see if they would show me the area, maybe, where this gentleman's person was sitting. Amazed, I looked at this one woman. She had this bright light around her. The rest of the room had darkened a bit, but she was lit up. I looked straight at her and said, "This is for you. Is your father on the other side?" "Yes," she replied. I told her, "I know this is for you. This is your dad." We started talking and he gave me more information and she said, "Yes, that is my father." I asked her about the socks. She paused for a moment and said, "You know, I just remembered he has these crazy colorful socks in his wedding picture! Everyone else is dressed up and he had these crazy socks on!" I asked her about the poofy rainbow and clouds. Again, she paused. She said, "I do see these poofy clouds and rainbow pictures when I am having a bad day, and I know everything will be alright. I know my father is near when I see them." I looked at her like, "This would have been nice to know ten minutes ago when I was flailing up here." I know, though, when we are not expecting to hear from someone or it might not be the information we are anticipating, we have what they call "psychic amnesia." We forget who we are, what our mothers' names are, how many siblings we have, and where we live. It seems the shock of actually getting a message overwhelms the senses and part of our brain shuts off. I understand this all too well!

Another very interesting thing happened that night. I was trying to connect the audience with this woman who said she was someone's sister. She was frantic to get the message to her person. I looked to the back of the room and that area lit up. I asked all of them standing back there if any of them had a sister who had a traumatic death. She kept telling me it was very traumatic and very sudden. They all shook their heads. I asked for more information from her. I was looking down getting more information and telling the audience what I was getting when the people in the back were calling to me. I looked up and there in the center of them stood a man. He was not there before. He said, "I have a sister who had a traumatic death." Stunned, I gave him the other clues she was giving me, and he said, "Yes, that is what happened. But I am not sure what is going on here. I just came in for some coffee." I said, "Do you have a minute, because obviously if your sister is going to work that hard to give you the message, it is important you hear it." A very shocked man who just came in for a quick cup of coffee to go listened as his sister gave him a very important message from the other side. I ended with,

"Your sister loves you very much, as demonstrated by what just happened here."

Even I could not believe this woman came to me knowing her brother would be stopping in so quickly and was able to relay enough information to have him say, "My sister had a traumatic death." The love they have for us goes so far beyond our comprehension. I learned so much that night. I learned it was not up to me, but it was up to Spirit to give the messages—I was just the messenger. I learned to what lengths our loved ones go to get our attention, and how much they will help me get *your* attention if you are in the audience. I learned my possibilities have no limits.

Talking with others that evening about the experience, none of them believed it was my first event. I owe that to my brilliant son, J.T., and Lightening McQueen. I still chuckle when I watch Disney Cars with Anthony, and I still use that visual when I get all tripped up over my limitations.

Fast Forward

There is so much we don't understand about our world and the world where our loved ones reside. I look back over the last few years and stand in amazement. What I have seen our loved ones do to get us the messages we so desperately need to hear, and the lengths to which they will go and push me so the messages are delivered astound me to this day.

I still have regular events at Anthology Book Company. I am still amazed at Spirit's clarity and eagerness to get those messages to loved ones in the audience. I am also still stunned at how easily the information comes if I get out of the way.

Now it is your turn.

I go back to my original message. I am not special. We are all psychic and we can all connect. The next chapters will go into detail and provide exercises so you can learn to connect, too!

Before you turn the page, tell yourself right now, "I can connect." The first step to connecting is believing! Now, let's begin.

THE BRIDGE

CHAPTER NINE
Where To Begin

I want to take some time to demystify what I do. I tune into energies. These energies could be your loved ones, or they could be your energies, depending on what type of reading I am doing. In a mediumship reading, I am asking for that loved one's energy to come close and communicate. In a psychic reading, I am tuning into that person's energy to see what that person might need to do to get on their path. Both types of readings are done in the same manner. I tune into the vibration of the energy.

Everything in the Universe is energy. We were energy before we came into these bodies, we are energy in these bodies, and we will be energy when we leave these bodies. One of most basic laws of science is the Law of the Conservation of Energy. Energy cannot be created or destroyed; it can only be changed from one form to another.

All energy also has a vibration. This vibration is the frequency and velocity of the energy. By tuning into the particular way in which that energy vibrates, or its energetic signature, I can receive information from it and about it.

What does this mean for you? It means you can also learn to tune in and receive.

The first thing I do when I sense an energy is determine its qualities. These are the questions I ask:

> Is it male or female?
> Is it vibrating at a fast rate or a slow rate?

Based upon these answers, I further determine what relation this energy has to my client—father, mother, sister, brother, child, etc.

The next step is to have the energy use whatever clairs are best to communicate more specific information. I can see, feel, hear and know information from the other side. Many energies prefer to use pictures to show me who they are or give me information specific to their loved one. Many like to talk to me, giving me the inflection of their voice or the characteristics of who they are by the way they speak. Others communicate through my physical body, or feeling, giving me impressions of how they felt physically before they passed. Some energies are very good communicators and some are not. Maybe they were shy when they were here, so they behave shyly and stay in the back of the room. Possibly, they might feel responsible for how they passed, so they will not come close, which makes clear communication difficult. When this occurs, I ask my guides to intervene and interpret for the energy so we can still receive the validation. We have to remember these are still people. They just don't have their bodies anymore. It seems more often than not, once I ask my guides to intervene and we find why they are staying away, they feel more comfortable coming closer.

One time in particular I felt such difficulty in the communication and I did not feel comfortable with what the energy was telling me. She was the daughter of a person I knew, and she almost seemed bothered I would ask her to come. Her mother was trying to make her be so specific, and the daughter I could see just rolled her eyes. She would say to me, "This is the most important thing my mom wants to know about me now?" This was the only time I could say I did not trust what I was hearing. I was also just beginning to do readings at this time, so my confidence was low. This spirit taught me a ton, though, about communication, as frustrating as it was at the time!

I bring this particular instance up because it is natural for us to want to receive specific information from our loved ones, something that would surely, beyond a shadow of doubt, come from our loved one. I have learned it is up to our loved ones on what they want to communicate, not us. Keep a very open mind and receive what they tell you. Putting limitations on the communication just leaves you frustrated and doubting. Part of this journey is to weed through the doubt and believe what you are receiving. Our loved ones will always give us something to identify who they are. Be open to what they give you. It will make the connection so much easier that way.

Breaking It Down

Let's take each of the items above and go a step deeper.

Clairs

We begin with the clairs. The clairs determine how we receive the information through our senses. The next chapter includes a quiz to help you determine which is your "dominant" clair, the one that is stronger than the others. I want to reiterate we all have all of these, but there will be one or two which are clearer than the others.

Clairsentience is "clear feeling." This is feeling in your physical body. It could be a vibration, goose bumps and/or aches. It could also be that "gut feeling" you have about someone or a situation.

Clairaudience is "clear hearing." This is hearing words in your head which may or may not be in your own voice. I am fortunate that I hear other people's voices so I can determine if I am speaking with a man, woman or child. For you, it might sound like your own thoughts, which makes it more challenging to distinguish if it is your own thoughts or whoever is communicating with you. I can say if you set your intention to hear, what you hear will be them, not you. Convincing yourself of this is the tricky part.

Clairvoyance is "clear seeing." This can be seeing energies as waves or outlines. It can also be seeing pictures in your mind. If you recall when my friend's father communicated with me, he used very clear pictures to get his messages to his daughter. Remember to avoid the "I have to see to be a medium" pitfall. Many mediums call themselves clairvoyants, which makes "regular folk" think you have to see spirits in order to be legitimate. I know this is what I thought when I began my journey. "If only I could see them…" This is not the case. Using any of the clairs to receive information is being a medium.

Claircognizance is "clear knowing." Those who have claircognizance as one of their clairs just receive information, as if it falls from the sky into their heads. They have no idea from where it comes. It is just there. Many men are claircognizant. They think they are just really smart to have all of these answers they just know, without realizing they are actually receiving this information from the Divine. This can also be very challenging to accept the information is coming from a Source outside of you because it seems so intrinsic. Many claircognizant individuals will need to work on trusting the information is truly from Spirit.

The next chapter will have specific exercises to help you identify and strengthen your clairs.

What is Vibration?

We all have what is called an "energetic signature." This is the frequency at which our energy vibrates. Even trees have a vibration. One of the first things a new psychic student learns is how to identify these vibrations.

High or Low

A high vibration is someone who has crossed to the other side and sees the bigger picture. A low vibration is an energy that has chosen to stay at the same vibrational level as when he or she was in a body. A low vibration does not see the bigger picture and is usually not trustworthy as a communicator. Many low vibrations believe they know what is best for us, but until they raise their vibration to see the bigger picture for them and us, they don't.

It is important to determine if the energy with which you are communicating is high or low in vibration. This will tell you whether the information is accurate and for your highest good.

When we first leave our bodies, we do not see the big picture yet. I find conversing with those recently departed is more like a conversation I would have with them when they were alive—there is still an ego attachment and a lot of emotion about what they did with their lives and the mistakes they made, or the mistakes others made against them. They do not see how it all fits into a plan and how they were part of that plan.

This is very important to remember since we still have the emotional attachments to our loved ones. If a loved one comes through and has any emotional response to questions, I know they have not been gone very long. I also know to take the information they give me with a grain of salt because, again, they are not seeing the picture from the higher perspective.

As time passes after we have left our bodies, our vibration gets higher and we can see the bigger picture. We learn more about who we are as spirits and how we are to help our loved ones on Earth. We understand the role we had in their lessons and the role they had in helping us learn our own lessons. We shed the hang ups, the attitudes, the disagreements and all emotion attached to what happened in our lives. We keep the love and the deepness of the relationships, especially with our families. We understand why we chose the mother and father we did in that life, and why our children are who they are. There is no time in the Spirit world, so this may take a few months to a few years, or longer, in Earth terms. There is no pressure to get it done, but we are gently encouraged by our helpers in the Spirit world and guides to do the work.

I want to be clear here because if you have lost a child, you worry about where he or she is. Children are never alone and seem to adapt much easier back into the Spirit world than adults. Their mission will be to help us through our process, whatever that may entail. They work very diligently to get us those signs and try to communicate to us through dreams, songs, animals and whatever other means they can.

The other circumstance about which parents worry is if their child left by their own choice and doing. I have communicated with many of these children—if you remember, my first contact with a child was Zane who left by suicide. These spirits might take a little longer raising their vibration, but I always hear they are exactly where they need to be. This means they are doing their work and learning about how their choice affected the plan and what they need to do to balance that energy. There are usually angels surrounding these souls and helping them assimilate back into the Spirit world. It is possible they need to isolate themselves for a time. They are always available to talk to their parents, though, so please do not worry you will not be able to contact them.

Those who have had a particularly difficult and painful life here on Earth might also choose to isolate for a time since that lifetime took its toll on the soul. Again, this is normal and there are no time constraints on when they need to reemerge. These souls might feel a bit farther away when we communicate with them, but again, they are always accessible.

Sometimes when people feel they have not led a good life or they have done things they should not have done, they are fearful of being sent to "hell." They will not go into the light, or "cross over" as we say. They will choose to stay at the energetic vibration they enter when the spirit leaves the body. These are the "ghosts" we speak of, like Ed. Since these energies really do not understand our path, it is very important to identify where they sit energetically. Therefore, I teach my students how to determine the energetic vibration of any energies they contact.

How to Identify High or Low

I suggest using a number line of sorts to help identify if the energy is at a high level or not. Again, those on the low side of the scale might not have the big picture and can give you information that is counter to your best interest. They might not be aware of this at the time and usually they just want to help. Nonetheless, you need to connect with energies at a five or above on a scale from zero to ten. This will ensure accurate information is exchanged. Zero refers to an energy that has not crossed over and feels very dense. You might get a feeling in the pit of your stomach, or just feel heaviness in your body, if you are a feeler. An energy at the five range will be lighter but still have a human quality to it. A ten energy is Archangel Michael who is very light and vibrates at a very fast rate. These energies are very high guides and know our contracts and what we are supposed to accomplish here, and will do what they can to assist us here on Earth.

Knowing if an energy is high or low will give you peace of mind and help you to trust what you are receiving.

There are exercises in the next chapter to practice this number line.

Reincarnation

Reincarnation is the belief that we have past lives, present lives and future lives. Too many psychics have told parents they cannot contact their children because they have reincarnated. This is one of those times my blood pressure goes up. This is absolutely not true. Our children will always be available to talk, whether they were one week old or ninety years old. We can even converse with those souls who were born sleeping and miscarried. How is this possible? Again, everything and everyone is energy. Anyone who has incarnated even for a few weeks is energy. If we know the laws of energy, it cannot be destroyed—it just converts to something else.

I know I have had past lives and have spent many of them with my current family members. We each have had different roles and lessons we provide for each other. My mother has been my mother in many lives and we are still teaching each other the same lessons. J.T. has been my son in many lives, also. We like the closeness of the mother-son bond. Similarly, John has been my son and Lacey has been my daughter and sister.

I know this because of the many past life regressions I have done with Brian Weiss and the information I can now access with my gifts. Learning about my past lives has healed and explained many of the experiences I have had. I do not dwell on them. I get the information and put it into my own reference. Learning about past lives should not make you feel more victimized or helpless. It should assist your healing and understanding of what you are doing now.

I have included past life regression information in the Resources section if you are interested in pursuing this for your own healing.

Infinite Energy

I remember clearly there was a time when I was told J.T. had to leave for a while to go "learn." I was devastated. I thought it would be forever until he came back and we could talk again. At the time I still knew so little about where J.T. was. He was "gone" for two days. When he came back in such a short time, I worried he came back for me and I was holding him from moving forward. He explained about how there is no time where he is, so two days or ten days, it had no reference where he was. He also told me he could be in more than one place at once. I wondered how my seven year old could do such a thing! I was reminded since he was not tied to Earthly time, he wasn't really seven anymore. Yes, he would still come to me in whatever form I needed and he would age for me if that helped me, but he was now an infinite soul. It took some time for me to assimilate this very foreign concept into my very logical mind.

Over the past four years, I have been given many of these types of messages. J.T. plants the idea by saying something a certain way, then he waits a couple of days and tells me the next piece. I think he knows my brain would implode if he gave me this information all at once! The concepts he explains to me are always mirrored in my readings or others with whom I speak, as if I needed the outside confirmation of what he told me. Of course, I need the validation! Sometimes I think my hearing has gone haywire! Hearing the same idea or information from another source is a great way for Spirit to say, "You see? We weren't messing with you. We really meant what we said!"

Helpers

Our helpers on this plane come in all shapes and sizes! I have two main categories, angels and guides, but see what fits for you.

I learned about angels from that experience with "Ed" but now I ask angels for daily assistance, from getting parking spots to raising my vibration to surrounding me with protection to boosting the energy in my body to assist healing from illness.

The word "angel" comes from "angelos" which means "messenger" in Ancient Greek. Angels are our infinite helpers. They assist us in living here on Earth. They protect us, they give us guidance, and they intervene when necessary to keep us out of harm's way. Unlike guides, angels bring us unconditional love, whereas spirit guides have personalities and often carry the traits they had when they were in bodies. Angels are a purer form of energy. They have very powerful energy, can be in many places at once and have an infinite energy source.

Angels have been recognized by many cultures, pre-dating the Christians. The Ancient Greeks had "gods" with angel-like qualities, such as Hermes who was considered a messenger of God, and in Rome, where he was called Mercury. The Vikings also had a messenger God called Hermod.

Guardian angels are those angels who stay with us and guide us gently through our lives. They will manifest in human form if they must to save us from something we did not agree would happen to us.

Archangels

The Archangels are special helpers. They have what I call "specialties." You can call on them at any time for any reason. They are infinite and are always full of love for you. You are never alone. You always have your Archangels. The main four with whom I work are:

> Michael, the protector
> Raphael, the healer
> Gabriel, the messenger
> Ariel, the soft one

For more information on the archangels, please read *Angels 101* by Doreen Virtue.

Spirit Guides

Spirit guides can come in many forms including human and animal.

The term "Spirit Guide" generally refer to those not in bodies who watch, teach, heal, and help you on our way. They have higher vibrations and see your paths in ways not possible from down here.

Spirit guides can go by many names. They are not attached to any names we call them. The names are really for us and not them.

Each guide generally comes to you for a specific purpose—creative abilities, healing issues, spiritual development, so it is possible for guides to come and go during your life depending on what their job assignment is for you.

Your guides do use signs to communicate with you. They might use birds, music, dreams, and toys, just to name a few, to get your attention. Enhancing your communication with your loved ones also gives you access to your guides. If talking with your guide interests you, feel free to use the exercises in the next chapter to assist you with this.

A great book about guides is *Ask Your Guides* by Sonia Choquette.

Animal Spirit Guides

An animal spirit guide could come to give you a quick message for the immediate issue at hand, or this guide might follow you on your path to help you discover who you are. Having an encounter with an animal guide will have a different feel to it. Maybe you have never noticed the hawks in the sky, and suddenly you look up and see one. Perhaps a rabbit runs in front of you as you walk or drive down the road. That is surely an animal guide with a message.

Great resources for animal spirit guides are any of the books by Steven Farmer.

Where Is Heaven?

Where is my child? Where is heaven? These were questions I asked my mentor, my guides and anyone else I could, trying to wrap my brain around this new reality in which I found myself. I am a very detail oriented person. By trade I was a Software

Quality Assurance Engineer prior to having children. I also did my fair share of process flows during some document management consulting prior to starting a family. These are left brain functions—the logical side. So much of what I was learning had nothing to do with logic and I had to accept that. My trust and faith in what I was learning was stretched to limits I did not know I had. I am an open minded person and accept others' truths. At the same time, I am very skeptical and relied on logic to be the ultimate authority.

Logic is not a word I would use for this world in which I now spend more time than not. The concepts I am sharing here are what I know to be true for me. I am always learning, though, and getting more pieces of the puzzle, so this concept might morph a bit here and there. At this point, this is what I understand about where J.T. and your loved ones reside. I am keeping this very basic so you can get the general concept. I invite you to put it through your own filters, use your own vernacular to understand this concept and explore with your loved ones to find your own version of the story.

There are different dimensions, as we call them. Different levels of energy reside at each of these levels. Here on Earth, we are in the third dimension, for the most part. We are dense because we are in bodies and live in on a dense planet, energetically speaking. Those who just leave their bodies go to the fourth dimension. They are still close enough to our dimension energetically, so we can sometimes see them and interact with them, especially those who are very sensitive. As we work on our stuff, we move to the higher dimensions—the fifth and above. It is with the fifth dimension and above where most of my communication takes place. I can and do converse with the fourth dimension, but I do not receive guidance from any energies in this dimension since they are not high enough to see my highest good.

There is not a "place" for these dimensions. My understanding is these dimensions occupy the same space. When I call to J.T., he has to come down to my vibration to communicate. He is not coming to a place; he is coming through the different levels of the dimensions to meet me where I am energetically.

This does not mean we are all on top of each other, though. There is plenty of room in our Universe for all of the energies to have the space they need to do whatever work that needs to be done!

Demystifying Meditation

Sometimes we make meditation too complicated. Simply, meditation is quieting the mind so your soul can speak. This can be done in so many ways. Taking walks in nature can be meditation. A soothing bath can be meditation. Sitting in a room with soft music and allowing your spirit to come to the surface and play for a while is absolutely meditation.

When I was learning to meditate, I preferred to have a guided meditation. This is where a narrator guides you to visualize certain places or things. I found it easier for my mind to quiet and my soul to speak during guided meditation. Others I know prefer walking meditation. It all depends on what resonates with your spirit. Try different ways. See which feel best. The important thing, of course, is to do it! The benefits are too numerous to list!

Meditation is not a technique but a way of life. Meditation means "a cessation of the thought process." It describes a state of consciousness, when the mind is free of scattered thoughts and various patterns. "Watching your breath" is meditation; listening to the birds is meditation. As long as these activities are free from any other distractions to the mind, it is effective meditation.

The word meditation, is derived from two Latin words: meditari (to think, to dwell upon, to exercise the mind) and mederi (to heal). Its Sanskrit derivation 'medha' means wisdom.

With a regular meditation practice, your connection to Source, Spirit, Creator, God—whatever you call that Infinite Energy—is enhanced and becomes clearer. Meditation is the key to Connection!

Meditation also raises your vibration, which is the frequency at which your soul vibrates. The higher the frequency of your energy, the easier it is to hear, see, feel and know the information from your loved ones and helpers.

The best time to meditate is in the morning, although anytime is good. Meditating in the morning sets the tone for the day. You begin your day at a higher vibration, which can make all the difference in how the rest of your day progresses. If you cannot find the time to meditate in the morning, just do it whenever you can. It only takes fifteen minutes to raise your vibration through meditation!

I have included a number of references in the Resources section to help you get started with your own meditative practice.

The bottom line, as I stated above, is to do it! Connecting with your loved ones depends on your ability to quiet your mind!

Questions

I frequently have events where I connect audience members with their loved ones on the other side. There are some questions I hear over and over. I include them here in case you had these questions also.

Q. Can my loved one hear me when I talk to him/her?
A. Absolutely! Whenever you talk to your loved one, think of him or her, or grieve, he or she is right beside you. Remember, they see you very differently now. The past is the past.

Q. Did he/she make it?
A. YES! Trust your loved one is exactly where he or she needs to be. We always have help and there is always someone close by to assist our loved ones if there is any confusion or complications at their passing.

Q. How do I know it is my loved one sending me a sign?
A. If the thought of your loved one crosses your mind, it is a sign. As soon as you think of your loved one, he or she is there. Sometimes, they give you the thought of them in conjunction with something else. Watch for the subtleties!

Q. Does my loved know I love him/her?
A. Of course! All your loved ones love you very much. That is the one thing we take with us: love.

Q. Are they finally out of pain?
A. Those of us who have had to watch a slow, painful passing with our loved ones are usually concerned about this. Once our loved ones cross over, all pain and suffering disappears. They have memory of it, but not the experience of it. As time goes on, they understand why they had to leave the way they did and how this affected others around them. Part of their work now is to help us come to terms with our experience of their pain and passing.

Q. I had an argument with my child right before he/she passed. Does he/she know I am sorry?
A. Your child sees you with love and understanding. It does not matter what happened here! Of course your child forgives you and wants you to let go of the guilt you feel about this situation. There are no exceptions to this, I can promise you. Forgive yourself. Your child already has!

Q. What did my loved one see when he/she passed?
A. This varies from person to person. Many will see Jesus if they expect to see Jesus. Many will see other loved ones who went before them. Many will just see the light and feel the incredible peace and love all around them. This peace and love is limitless and gives a feeling of safety and security. We usually recognize it as familiar—we are home.

Q. My loved one was very mean to me. I am not sure I want to even talk to him/her.
A. Your loved one now sees his/her part in what happened. They are no longer in the emotion or ego of the situation. Sometimes, they might come through with this personality so you recognize them, but they will immediately show you how much they love you.

An example of this occurred during one of my Connecting to the Other Side events. A man came through telling me he was the father of one of the audience members. He was looking for his son. I described him and a picture he showed me. It was of a boy with a German shepherd. I could see the picture so clearly, but no one was claiming the man. Finally, a woman raised her hand and said, "I think you are talking about me." She clearly was not the man's son. I looked at her puzzled. She told me her father wanted boys. He had all girls but named them boy names. Her name was Jackie. She told me he was not the most pleasant father, and this was verified by the man who was telling me some things which were certainly not pleasant. I was having a conversation with him in my head telling him he'd better shape up or I will stop the connection. He told me, "She won't believe it's me if you don't tell her what I said." I understood what he meant. If your father was a mean man and the spirit who claimed to be him was nice, would you believe it was him? No. He had to be nasty in order for her to believe it really was him. He softened immediately and started giving me messages from the heart, transforming into the soul he truly is now.

I was so compelled by Jackie's dad I looked her up on Facebook that evening. I had a feeling I would find the picture her dad showed me of Jackie and the dog. Sure enough, there it was. I was astounded at how clear her father was. Jackie had very short blonde hair and was dressed in overalls standing beside her dog, just like her father claimed!

I learned more about Spirit that night. "Things are not always as they seem! Keep an open mind and the answers will be clear," they tell me. Words to live by, if you ask me.

Chapter Ten
Connecting Exercises

Exercise 1: The Steps to Connecting

Step One: Believe You Can Connect

The first step in learning to connect is to believe you can! We do this by using affirmations. An affirmation is a statement of how we want things to be. It is very important, though, to phrase it as if we already have it in our reality. The greatest example I have of this is when I was trying so desperately to *see*. I wanted to see energies and be clairvoyant. In the training groups I would say, "Oh, I can't see." I realized of course I couldn't see because I didn't believe I could see! When this was pointed out to me, I changed it to, "I am working on seeing." Shortly after that time I had that experience with my friend's father. You must believe you can connect.

So right now, take a very deep breath. Breathe all the way into your abdomen and then exhale completely. Now say, "I *can* connect with my angels, guides and loved ones." Say it again, "I *can* connect with my angels, guides and loved ones." I want you to remember this as you go through these exercises. When you start to doubt yourself and get discouraged, say it again. "I *can* connect with my angels, guides and loved ones."

Remember, we are all psychic. We can all connect. I am not special. I was a stay at home mom with three young children. If *I* can learn how to do this, so can you! You *can* connect with your angels, guides and loved ones.

Step Two: Clearing and Protecting

I want you to feel safe and protected whenever you connect. Fear holds us from moving. Learning how to clear and protect yourself and your environment will help you get to the next level so you feel free to move!

There are so many ways to do this clearing. I use the angels to help me clear my energy and the energy in my house and clear out any stale or unwanted energy, wherever it may originate.

Asking for Archangel Michael's assistance is extremely effective and easy. It is all about intentions. So make sure your intentions are clear no matter what you are intending! Archangel Michael is so close to that God energy and is the highest on the vibrational scale. I call him the Cosmic Bouncer since he will remove any energy you ask him to remove. Trust him; he gets the job done!

The first thing I want you to do is take a few deep breaths. Center yourself and open up to the Divine. Then say this prayer:

> "Dear Archangel Michael, please vacuum out my house, each and every room, removing any energies that are not for our highest and purest good, or my Divine purpose. Please use the high setting and replace any energy removed with your light and love. Thank you so much."

You should feel a lift of energy in your house after you do this. If you wish to seal your house so only high vibrational energies are allowed through the door, say this prayer:

> "Dear Archangel Michael, please seal this house, all entrances, doors, windows, ceiling, floor, wall to wall so only high vibration is allowed inside. All other vibrations must stay outside this house. Thank you so much!"

Once you feel the process is complete, say this prayer:

"Dear Archangel Michael, please vacuum any energies out of my body, my aura, my energy fields and centers that are not for my highest and purest good or for my Divine purpose. Please use the (high/medium/low) setting and replace any energy removed with your light and love. Thank you so much."

The settings are how slowly or quickly Archangel Michael removes the energies. Play with it and see what fits for you.

You should feel lighter after this is done.

You can do this anytime you feel you might have picked up some lower energy somewhere, and for your house whenever you feel it needs it.

If you wish to take it to the next level and have Archangel Michael protect you from lower vibrations from now on, this is the prayer for that:

"Dear Archangel Michael, please be my protector from this day forward. Surround me with your love and light and allow only high vibrational energies to be close to me. Thank you so much!"

That's it! If you ever feel any fear around anything, call to Archangel Michael, and he will be there.

A note about this last part, you might still feel different energies around you since we do still live in the third dimension. Archangel Michael protects them from attaching to you (unless you allow this), but he cannot keep them out of your existence.

The more you raise your vibration, though, the higher vibrations will surround you and the lower vibrations will seem farther away. So keep those vibrations high! Step five will discuss ways to keep your vibration high.

Step Three: Breathe

Each day, take time to breathe deeply. Close your eyes and breathe into your stomach. Hold for a moment, then release. Do this for at least five breaths. The more you stop and breathe, the easier it will be to learn to meditate.

There is a difference between "normal" breath and true breathing.

True breathing is also called "belly breathing". For most of us, our breath stops right at our heart center. Stop for a minute and pay attention to your breath. Your lungs are actually below your heart center. When you belly breathe, your lungs should fill with air, making your "belly" rise. Your exhale should be full, letting all the air out. Using this breathing technique brings oxygen into the body, releasing stress and raising your vibration. It is so simple you can use it anytime and anywhere.

> Blow your nose if it feels stuffy
> Sit or lie down in a comfortable position. Either works for this exercise.
> Close your eyes
> Place your hand on your stomach
> Inhale through your nose all the way into your stomach so it expands
> Slowly breathe out through your nose, exhaling fully and completely
> Keep breathing in and out slowly for a few minutes, making sure your breath reaches all the way into your belly.

Note: Your chest should not move much. You might try putting your other hand on your chest to be sure your breath is mostly going into your belly. Don't worry if you start yawning. Your body naturally breathes into the belly when you yawn. Feel the yawn and see if this is true.

Breathing deeply is important because it is how our senses open. By breathing deeply and deliberately, we open our senses to receive information we might not receive otherwise.

"Minding" your breath is also very helpful for meditation. Meditation is a fancy word for quieting the mind to let the spirit speak. When I say "minding" your breath, I mean to be conscious of it. Consciously breathe in and consciously breathe out. Some use a count of 4 to bring awareness to their breath. This would look something like this:

> Take a deep full breath. As you breathe in, count to four slowly
> Exhale fully as you count to four again.
> Continue this for at least 10 full breaths

As you are breathing on the four counts, keep focused on a single image in your mind. A big oak tree would be good if you cannot think of anything else. If other thoughts come in, push them aside and bring the oak tree or other image back to your awareness.

After you complete this, concentrate on your body. How does it feel? It should feel relaxed and energized.

Step Four: Quiet the Critical Thinker

The next step to connecting is to begin the process of training your mind, or as I call it, the critical thinker, to play along. Our minds are incredibly powerful. They keep us safe from harm and they create logical steps for us to follow to get from point A to point B. The problem is connecting to the other side is not logical. The mind does not know what to do with this, and it will tell you how crazy it is to think you could even do this. What the mind does not know is we are not *thinking* our way through this. We are using our creative side, the right brain, in this process. The left brain usually does not like this, though, and may try to sabotage your progress. I know for me, one of the hardest things I had to do was quiet my critical thinker.

The simplest way to quiet the critical thinker is to meditate. Now, I can speak from experience when I was told I had to meditate to be able to talk to my son, I wanted to quit right there. When I was 30, I took a meditation class. Disaster! I tried and tried, but I could not just sit there and clear my mind. I would think of the grocery list or did I feed the dog—all those mundane things which occupy our thoughts. When it was clear to me, though, I needed to meditate to hear J.T. I decided to give it another try. This time I used a guided meditation. In a guided meditation, you concentrate on a soothing voice and your left brain is listening to the words and instructions while the right brain is working on connecting. By using a guided meditation, I was able to satisfy my left brain by giving it something to do— it had to listen to the words of whoever was guiding me. It was then when I learned I really could meditate and I became a very successful meditator!

It is critical you make time each and every day to develop your meditative practice. This is challenging at first for everyone. Once I started the routine, I noticed such a difference in my outlook on life and my ability to connect became much easier. It took some time to do this, though. You must make it a priority if you want to connect with your loved ones.

There are many ways to meditate, also. You do not have to use a guided meditation. You can do what they call a walking meditation where you take a walk and just observe all that is around you. Really observe it. See how crisp the leaves on the trees are. Smell the air. Let your senses take in everything. This is meditation! Another form of meditation is gardening, or painting pottery or anything creative. I have a student who meditates as she crochets. The hand movement as she crochets is enough to keep her left brain busy as her right brain takes her on that journey to meet her guides, angels and loved ones.

Do whatever works for you, but make sure you do it. Meditation is the key to connecting! It quiets the critical thinker and allows your right brain to take you on that journey to connect with your Infinite Support System.

Ways to quiet that critical thinker include:

A walk in nature.

Meditation.

A quiet drive in the country.

Listening to calming music.

Doing anything creative.

Play around and see what works for you.

For more meditation resources, please see the Resources section in the back of this book.

Step Five: Keep Your Vibration High

The vibration is the rate at which everything in the Universe runs. If you remember in the beginning I said we were all energy. Each of us runs at a certain vibrational rate. Being in bodies here on the planet, our energy is a lot denser than our loved ones who do not have bodies anymore. The best way to connect with them is to get as close to their vibration as possible. Things you can do to raise your vibration to meet those on the other side are meditation, Reiki, setting positive intentions and prayer, smiling, laughing, walking in nature, petting a dog or a cat. Believe it or not, all of these things raise your vibration. You want to get as high as you can because the higher you get, the clearer you will receive. It is important to note, though, that having a high vibration does not mean you have to be out of your body. I spent most of my life outside of my body until I went into psychic training. As counterintuitive as it sounds, you need to also be well grounded to be a good receiver. So you need to stay in your body, but raise the vibration of your body, not just your spirit, to be a good receiver.

Step Six: Ground

Grounding is a process of planting your feet firmly on the ground and calling in all your energy to be in your body. Google defines grounding as "grounded - Of or pertaining to an electrical conductor which is connected to earth; earthed; Not allowed to fly." What a great definition! For us humans, it is a "direct electrical connection to the earth." What this does for us is pull us back into our bodies. We spend a lot of time in our heads, thinking about what we are doing next, what we will eat for dinner, how we will pay the bills. By connecting with the earth, we pull our awareness away from the mind and into the center of our bodies. Our heart center and power center are where all the connecting to Spirit begins. If there are pieces of us floating around and somewhat attached but not really present, it is very difficult to have awareness to the signs and communication around you, not only from this world, but also from the other side. By being fully present, we can observe so much more in the world around us.

The easiest way to ground is to sink your feet into the earth, literally. This may not be possible year round, however, so below are other methods of grounding which have worked very well for me.

First, take a deep cleansing breath. Breathing clears out the cobwebs. Then imagine there are roots going from the bottom of your feet all the way to the center of the earth and then imagine these roots attaching themselves there. If you are feeling particularly flighty a certain day and having a hard time feeling rooted, take those roots and imagine you are wrapping them around the core of the earth a few times. If you still are not feeling grounded, imagine a cord, called a grounding cord, coming from the base of your spine. It goes all the down to the center of the earth and attaches there, too. If you can't seem to make it to the core of the earth, get as deep as you can. The point is to feel sturdy, like a tree.

There are other ways to ground you can incorporate in your day. Go for a walk in nature. This can be a form of meditation. Gardening is another wonderful way to ground. In the winter, it might be a challenge, but there are always ways to play in the dirt even in the winter!

You might need to practice grounding. When I was first learning how to ground and connect, I put notes around the house, in my car, everywhere, reminding me to ground. Sitting at red lights, I would check my grounding. Again, because I enjoyed not being present in my body, I would fly out. I had to really practice being in my body and grounding. So don't get discouraged if you feel you are not getting that connection to the earth. Just keep trying.

Step Seven: Setting Intention

Setting intention is a little different than saying our affirmation that we can connect. It is telling the Universe, guides, angels and our loved ones what we expect from this experience.

I use the following prayer of intention and suggest you use something similar each time you begin any psychic or connecting exercises:

"My prayer of intention is that I clearly hear, feel, see and know all that I need to know today. My intention is also that I boost my abilities to receive from my angels, guides and loved ones. I am a clear receiver and the information flows easily. Only positive loving high vibration energies are allowed to communicate with me right now, and I invite you in now, all those who wish to assist me today. I know I am always protected. I am so grateful to be able to do this."

This prayer has all of the points we want to include whenever we are connecting: What we expect from ourselves and our helpers; only high vibration can connect with us; we know we can receive clearly; we are protected; we are grateful for the connection. If there is someone in particular with whom you wish to connect, invite them in. It is always a great idea to include gratitude in your prayers. God, Source, The Universe, the One, whatever you call that Divine energy, responds very well to gratitude!

Step Eight: Journal

It is difficult for some of us to perceive those hunches we get, those signs we get, and the knowing we have is really from Spirit/Source. Journaling these synchronicities is a great way to quiet the critical thinker and realize you really are getting information from the Divine and your loved ones.

Keep a notepad in the car, on the coffee table and on your office desk. Each time something happens where you feel it might have been a sign or some other intuitive event, write down the date, time and what happened. You might be surprised at how often these things happen! Even if you aren't sure, write it down anyway.

I also encourage all my students to journal all experiences they have in meditation. This is the way we integrate the left and right brains and get everyone on board with what we are doing. Writing down who you met and what happened during your meditations tells your left brain this a real event. Refrain from writing anything like, "I don't know if this is real or not, but..." as this will perpetuate the paradigm that you cannot connect. Treat all experiences as real encounters with the other side.

Step Nine: Take Time For You

Take at least 15 minutes a day, preferably more, which is devoted to something you enjoy doing! Something creative! Fill yourself up. This might seem pretty obvious, but how many of us do really schedule "me" time? It is essential to connecting.

We all have value, but many of us place our own value below those of others. If you say to God and the Universe, "I am not as valuable as..." then we are saying we don't "deserve" connection. Know you are very valuable and deserve time just for you. It is not selfish. Schedule it into your day—15 minutes at least. Tell the Universe you do value yourself!

Step Ten: Medications

Certain medications that involve changing the chemistry of the brain can interfere with communication with our loved ones. This does not mean you stop taking them! Just have the awareness that it might play into your ability to receive clearly.

I am not advocating you stop any medications. I just want you to be aware that antidepressants and other medications that change brain chemistry may interfere. It does not mean they do in all cases. Your loved ones will do everything they can to counter the medication's effects, but you need to be aware these medications do interfere with your ability to meditate and clear your mind. If you have a naturopath in your area, they may have alternatives to the common prescribed medications for depression, ADD, ADHD and anxiety which will help for clearer communication.

Step Eleven: Lighten The Load

We carry around energy that is not ours and weighs us down. This makes it harder for our loved ones to "reach down" to us.

Lesson one for empaths (those who feel others' pain and emotions): Protect, protect, protect.

Others will gladly give you their "stuff." It is not yours to take. It is imperative that you protect yourself from others' pain and emotions because it will drain your energy. The only energy you should have is your own. This does not mean you can't help others. What it means is that you will be clear and have boundaries so you can help much more than if you enmesh with other people.

Before you leave the house, each and every time, state this intention: "I take only my energy with me. Only my energy is allowed to be in my aura, body and spirit. All other energies return to Mother Earth or to the spirit to whom it belongs. I am fully protected from others' energy." You can envision a golden light filling your body and your aura also. Gold is the light of protection.

Dumping Others' Stuff:

If you feel you have picked up another person's energy, ground and send it down your grounding.

Next, say "I release all the energy in my body, spirit and aura which are not mine or not for my highest and purest good. These energies are sent down my grounding and accepted by Mother Earth. She uses this energy to create many beautiful things."

Step Twelve: Forgiveness

Our loved ones have a very unique perspective. They hold no grudges; they have no anger or disappointment. They only have love for us and want the best for us.

No matter how your loved one passed, if you feel any guilt around how they lived or left, release it. They have already forgiven everything that happened in their life. It's very important that you forgive what happened also.

Guilt and non-forgiveness are very low vibration emotions. They stifle you and your ability to move forward with whatever you need to do in this life. There are many times we wish we were with our loved ones on the other side. The truth is we must do what we came here to do. Our loved ones are there to help us and absolutely do not want to see us suffering because of guilt or non-forgiveness.

This can have an effect on whether you receive messages from your loved one, not because they are mad at us, but because your negative emotions are blocking the messages.

Step Thirteen: Gratitude

We touched on this a little when we were setting our intentions. I know this can be hard to do at times. When you lose a loved one, why should you be grateful? Having gratitude for the little things raises your vibration. The higher your vibration, the closer you are to your loved ones.

One way to incorporate gratitude into your daily routine is to have a gratitude journal. Every day write down at least one thing for which you are grateful. If that feels too daunting, just say at least thing for which you are grateful when you are brushing your teeth. Maybe gratitude for having teeth?

Step Fourteen: Heal Your Heart

What a tall order for some of us! When I asked J.T. about this as I was gathering information for this book, I said, "Geesh! You are talking about many of us who have had to say goodbye to children. How are we supposed to do this?" He answered "One piece at a time." We may never be fully healed—that's not what this is asking. We do need to take steps to heal piece by piece, though. That might mean allowing yourself to grieve. Many of us stuff our grief. You must grieve. You must mourn. That is the bottom line.

Another way to heal your heart is by looking at other wounds in your heart other than grief. How do you feel about yourself? Do you love yourself? Do you believe you are a child of God? If you don't, what do you need to feel like you have that Divine spark within you that can never be extinguished?

Only you can answer these questions. Take some time and be honest with yourself. How can your loved one get through to you if you do not feel worthy?

Step Fifteen: Practice!

Practice makes perfect! The exercises in this chapter need to be done over a period of time before you might see results. For some, it just clicks and just by reading this today, you have opened the door to communicating with the other side and are on your way! For others, there might be some blocks in your way. Don't get discouraged! Our Infinite Support System wants this communication with us! They will do everything they can to help you! Make sure you give yourself enough time and permission to do this. You and your loved ones will be very glad you did.

Exercise 2: How Do You Receive Information?

Answer Yes or No to the following questions to see how you receive information through your senses. Whichever section has the most "yes" answers determines your "dominant clair." We always work with the dominant clair first to communicate successfully with the other side. Your other clairs will come in the picture soon enough!

> Are you a "seer" (clairvoyant):
> When you first encounter someone new, do you first notice how they look? Yes   No
> Can you see pictures in your mind when you close your eyes? Yes   No
> When someone is telling you a story, do you see it in your mind? Yes   No
> Do you see colors around people? Yes   No
> Do you see colors when you close your eyes? Yes   No
>
> Do you "hear" (clairaudience)?
> Have you heard voices in your head you knew were not yours? Yes   No
> When you ask a question, do you hear the answer in your head? Yes   No

Do your ears ring? Yes No

Are you a "feeler" (clairsentience)?
When you enter a room, do you feel the vibes in the room before you see anyone? Yes No
When you talk to someone who feels down, do you start to feel down, while they start feeling better? Yes No
Do you feel tightness in your body when someone else has an ailment in their body? Yes No
Do others dictate what your mood is by the way they feel? Yes No

Do you just "know" what you know (claircognizance)?
Have you ever just known something without ever learning it or hearing it? Yes No
Have you ever had someone ask you a question and without even thinking about it, you knew the answer, and you knew it was the true answer? Yes No
Do answers or solutions drop into your head as if they have been there all along? Yes No

Based on the number of Yes answers, use the next sections to learn how to enhance your dominant clair. This is the clair that receives information the clearest. It does not mean you will never have the other clairs, because we all have them. We work with your dominant clair first, though, and strengthen it, so whichever section has the most Yes answers indicates where you begin.

Exercise 3: Strengthen Your Clairs

Note: If during any of these exercises you sense information that has a negative tone, this is not from your angels and guides. It could be your mind and the old tapes playing from your childhood or programming, or it could be something else. Regardless, stop the exercise and set your intention again. Ask for your angels to come closer and begin the exercise again. If it still feels negative, ask your angels to help you remove the negative energy, wherever it is coming from, and then resume the exercise.

Clairvoyance

Clairvoyance is sometimes misconstrued as being able to see spirits. Yes, this is part of it, but more than this, it is seeing images or visions in your mind.

Clairvoyance is your dominant clair if you see people's energy, see auras, see mists in the context that they are souls or spirits. You are also clairvoyant if you see through your mind's eye. This would be if you are given pictures by those on the other side to identify who they are. You see it in your mind, like a movie or pictures.

Keep a journal and include all the times you are given "pictures", or the times when you see energy.

You can also journal any symbols Spirit uses to convey a message, like "roses" might mean love or an anniversary, balloons might mean birthday, etc.

If seeing is your dominant clair, close your eyes right now. What do you see? Do you see an image or colors? You can practice your clairvoyance by asking your Infinite Support System to open this clair even more and give you pictures and colors when you are meditating. Another way to practice is to sit and observe a tree. Trees have auras. See if you can "see" the aura of the tree. How far out does it extend from the tree? Does it have color or is it white? Practice with other items in nature, also. Every living thing has energy around it!

Clairaudience

Your dominant clair is clairaudience if you hear answers from Spirit. This might seem like your own voice, but the inflection and/or words might not be what you would ordinarily say.

An example of this is when I was on the phone with the medium who said, "You are clairaudient. You can hear them." I said, "No, I can't." Suddenly in my head another voice said, "Yes, you can." I knew these were the high guides with whom she was speaking. They felt very powerful and I knew they knew what they were talking about! So I said, "I guess I can!"

I also had Archangel Ariel by my side 24/7 to help me with my fear of the lower energies. Whenever I would call out to her, "Are you there?" a soft loving voice would respond, "Yes, I am here."

It can happen just like that. You hear "Mommy" and turn around to find no one is there. That could be your child on the other side calling to you. Maybe you hear your name in your head, in your voice or someone else's. This could be a loved one or guide.

You can tell it is Spirit and not just your mind by the way in which the questions are answered. Spirit will not say anything negative or make you feel like you did something wrong. Spirit is loving and understanding. Sometimes, as with Archangel Michael, the voice is powerful and commanding, but again, they will never ask you to do anything that would put you in harm's way or say anything to make you feel badly about something you did.

How to tell whether the "voices" in your head are yours or not:

One trick I learned which helped was to ask my questions aloud. That way the answer didn't sound like it was coming from me. For whatever reason, doing this differentiated my voice from whoever was answering. I also suggest sticking to questions that can be answered "yes" or "no" in the beginning. This makes it very simple. Also, if the voice sounds critical in any way, remember, it is not coming from Spirit. That would happen to me occasionally where my critical mind got in the way and thought "she" knew the answer, but there was a feel about it which I knew was not coming from that "higher" place. I told her to be quiet and asked the question again. Because I doubted myself so much in the beginning, I usually asked the same question different ways numerous times. You will drive yourself crazy doing this! Try to refrain from this. Trust. This is an exercise of trust.

To enhance your clairaudience:

First ask for this clair to be enhanced! A very simple prayer is "I ask that my ability to hear Spirit, God, the Universe (whatever you call this realm) be opened. Please allow my hearing to be clear and concise. Thank you so much for this opportunity to hear you." Another way to put it is, "I know my hearing of Spirit is getting clearer and more concise." Then believe in yourself. Believe you can hear. We all have that connection to the other side.

Another way to enhance clairaudience is to do automatic writing. With this technique, you are writing what you are hearing, not what you are thinking. Automatic writing means different things to different people. I will tell you how I do automatic writing and then you can look up other ways on the internet if you would like to see what works best for you. I meditate first, then set up my protection and set intention:

> "My intention for this automatic writing session is that I hear clearly and that only the person/energy I ask to come talk with me is allowed to come. I know I am protected during this session and I thank my helpers for this assistance."

Then I sit at my computer with an open word processing document. I ask a question, such as, "Who is here with me?" and then I type the answer. My eyes are closed and I am just typing what I hear in my head. I ask more questions and type the answers. This is a great way to receive messages and get the critical thinker out of the way!

Clairsentience

Clairsentience is when you can feel your loved one is around, but don't have any "proof" of it. You just feel it. This could be through sensing they are near, or it could be via a sensation in your body. During those first months after J.T. left, I would feel this tingling sensation on my left hip when I cried. I thought I was going crazy, until someone told me it was J.T. giving me a hug. I thought about it and the tingling was at the right height where his arms would reach around me.

If you *feel* before you see, know or hear, then clairsentience is your dominant clair. Spirits use my clairsentient abilities to get my attention. They send a vibration somewhere on my body, like a tickling feeling. I also can feel how a person passed, or maybe if the person smoked or had chronic pain, because that pain occurs in my body, even though it is not mine. It is also the feeling that you are being watched, but turn around and no one is there.

Enhancing your Clairsentient abilities:

The first exercise is to see what you feel in your body as "yes" answers and what you feel in your body as "no" answers. You are creating the way in which your guides, angels and loved ones will communicate with you.

Get comfortable, ground and clear yourself of any thoughts or energies that are not for your highest good. Say prayer of intention such as, "I ask that my feelings be heightened for this exercise and that the answers I receive are clear and concise. Help me to raise my vibration to meet those of my angels and my guides. Only high vibration loving energies are allowed to answer me. Thank you for your assistance." Then, ask yourself a question aloud to which you know the answer is yes, i.e., my name is _____. Feel into that answer as it sets in your body. Does it feel light or have a certain texture to it? Do you feel "yes" somewhere in your body?

Then ask yourself a question to which you know the answer is no, i.e., I am a male/female in this lifetime (using the opposite of what you are, of course). What does that feel like? Is it heavier, does it tingle somewhere? Mark the differences down in your journal (you all should have journals for this stuff!) and keep practicing until you are sure how "yes" and "no" feel in your body.

Next is identifying male energy vs. female energy.

There is a distinct difference between male energy and female energy. If you are a feeler, it is important for you to identify whose energy is in front of you.

Follow the same instructions with the grounding and prayer of intention. We are also asking for protection since we will be calling in some angelic helpers. Protection prayer is something like this, "I ask that I am fully protected and that only high vibration, loving energies are allowed to come near me." I also usually call on Archangel Michael to oversee this exercise.

Get cozy and ask your "yes" and "no" questions to make sure you are tuned in. Once you feel like you can tell the difference between the "yes" and "no", ask for Archangel Ariel to stand in front of you. Her energy is incredibly light, yet powerful. Make note of anything you feel about her energy.

Thank Archangel Ariel and now ask for Archangel Michael to come stand in front of you. What do you notice that is different? He should also feel very high vibration, but there is a different frequency with him. See if you can compare the two in your mind.

Thank Archangel Michael and close the session.

It is all about becoming clearer and raising our vibration so you can trust what you are getting.

Practice this every day.

A special note to you feelers: You are magnets for energy. As I said before, you absorb other people's energy and definitely need to set intention around how much of that energy comes into your space. Before your feet hit the floor in the morning, set your intention about what you are going to "feel" for that day. My intention is this: "My energy is mine and their energy is theirs." You must keep the boundary between you and others. You do not need to take away people's pain by absorbing it into your body. It is their pain and they need to deal with it. Now, many of you feelers are already healers. I would encourage each of you to find a healing modality that fits for you and learn it. This will help you to heal others without taking it on yourself. It is not healthy to take on other people's stuff.

Claircognizance

Claircognizance is "clear knowing". This is when you have a thought, and you just know it is true, but you have no idea why you know it.

This one can make you feel like you are going crazy. Many people are claircognizant and just pass it off as being smart. What is happening, really, is that Spirit gives them information as thoughts. It is very elusive because you can't really put your finger on why you know what you know, just that you know that it is the truth. You will begin to learn how to discern from where the information is coming through practice.

Some examples of claircognizance are:

Knowing driving directions without ever having been there

Knowing the answer to a question you would have no way of knowing

Knowing exactly what to tell a person without really knowing the person

Knowing someone is lying to you

Knowing events will occur before they actually occur

To tell the difference between your thoughts and "inspired" thoughts, ask yourself:

Is this something I would know?

Is there any ego attachment to it?

Does this seem like it is from me or my spiritual guidance?

The differences can be subtle, but with practice, you will be able to tell the difference. Another exercise to enhancing your knowing is to meditate and then ask your angels to come very close and to communicate very clearly. Then ask a question to which you would not know the answer. You might be surprised at what comes into your head!

Exercise 4: Who's Talking?

Fear is a four letter word. I have given you many ways to feel safe and protected as you begin connecting with your loved ones, angels and guides. This next exercise will take it to the next level. We will work on identifying the vibrational level of any energies with whom you have contact.

In Chapter Nine, I referenced a number line system I use to determine where an energy sits vibrationally. Use your dominant clair for this exercise and practice this often.

> The scale is from zero to ten:
> 0 – 3: Energies who have not crossed into the light
> 4 – 6: Our loved ones on the other side
> 7 – 10: Our high guides and helpers who have unconditional love for us and understand our path

To practice this, say your prayer of intention and protection, and then ask Archangel Michael to come to you. Using your dominant clair, determine where he sits on the number line. If you are a seer, you might see the number in your mind. If you are a feeler, you will feel his vibration. If you hear, he will tell you in your mind. If you are a knower, you will know the answer. He should be a ten.

Next, ask for a high guide or angel to come. This energy should be somewhere between seven and ten. Then, ask for a loved one to come. Your loved one should be somewhere between four and six. If they just left their body, it might be close to a three. I do not suggest you ask a low vibration at this stage of your training. You should only communicate with those energies that vibrate at a five or higher. Identifying with whom you are communicating will make all the difference in your connections. You will know exactly what kind of energy is with you, allowing you to open up your senses and trust the information you receive. Practice this as often as you can! You will be surprised at how successful you feel when you know with who you are connecting!

CHAPTER ELEVEN
The Culmination Point

Much of this book has been chronological. I felt something was missing from this book as I was finishing it. "What did I forget?" I asked myself. I looked back over the chapters and felt the information I gave was complete, so why do I feel there is something missing?

I realized it will be five years at the end of this month since J.T. left. There is no coincidence I am finishing this book at this time of the year. Each year that passes I feel closer to my son and more in line with my purpose. Last year on J.T.'s angelversary, we had a balloon release at the cemetery for him. We have had one every year since he left and the same people come each year. Last year after we released all the balloons, J.T. told me he wanted to address the group. We were all attentive and ready to hear what he had to say. He began, "This will be the last balloon release you have for me on this date." As I spoke the words, inside I was dying. This was my tribute to my son! Why would he not want us to do this?

He continued, "I want a different relationship with each of you. I will come to you and show you who I am now. This is what I want you to remember, not my body in the ground."

I understood what he was saying. He had been working with me for three years on this concept. He is so much more than just the little boy who graced us with his infectious belly laugh, amazing humor and incredible kindness to others. He is an infinite spirit now and capable of more than we can understand with our limited cognitive abilities.

Here we are another year down the road. So much has happened; I can't begin to tell you the presence my son has in my life now. He shows me his immenseness these five years later in ways I could never have imagined. The strength he brings to me and my family each day astounds me. The people he has brought into my life, and those he has helped remove, are all part of such a greater plan. I trust him implicitly and do exactly what he instructs me to do. He sees my plan. He is my teacher, my friend, my guide, my strength, my solace, and so much more. He will always be my son first and foremost, but that role is very limiting, he tells me!

I invite you to open your hearts to your loved ones and let them know you are ready for this journey. They want to show you what J.T. has shown me. They no longer have any limits. They no longer worry about where they are going or where they have been. They are infinite, just like my little boy (he chuckles when I call him that).

The culmination point is where we meet our loved ones for who they are now. It takes time and patience to understand and integrate this concept into our perception of how things are. For me, I cannot imagine a greater gift J.T. could give me than to give me this glimpse of infiniteness.

I will be with him again one day in that place we call Heaven. For now, I continue my work with him by my side, with gratitude and love for all he has given me, and all he is now. I am one of the lucky ones, I tell him. He smiles and tells me, "No, I am." We argue back and forth a bit, but we know we couldn't do this work without each other.

Know you can connect and know your loved ones want this connection. The time is now. Use it.

J.T.'s parting words as I write this? "How Do You Like Me Now?" by Toby Keith, J.T.'s favorite country artist, just came on the radio. I believe that says it all!

MEMORIAL SECTION FOR OUR ANGELS

This section is dedicated to all of those children who left before us. We know you have so much to teach us! Thank you for being our kids!

Aaron Earnest Roy Cann ♥ 5/19/97 ~ 5/20/97
Aaron Edward Lawrence ♥ 5/29/90 ~ 7/20/10
Aaron Marsh ♥ 8/31/85 ~ 11/9/10
Aaron Robert Simon ♥ 7/5/85 ~ 1/3/07
Abigail Georgina Cann ♥ 5/19/97 ~ 5/23/97
Abigail Hope Worley ♥ 6/13/09 ~ 4/28/10
Abigale Lynn Nobel ♥ 1/4/11
Adam John Vardon ♥ 8/18/93
Adam Lee Josiah Murphy ♥ 8/05/94 ~ 2/28/06
Adam Michael Encarnacion ♥ 10/24/86 ~ 11/28/02
Adam William Hess ♥ 5/19/85 ~ 9/4/09
Addison Lynn Day ♥ 12/12/10 ~ 4/29/11
Addyson Ryleigh ♥ 2/25/11 ~ 3/5/11
Adin Lee MacPhail ♥ 2/24/07~11/26/08
Adrian Hightower ♥ 10/3/91 ~ 11/26/20
Adrianna May Potts ♥ 11/13/98 ~ 8/29/10
Agnetha Joe-Leighe Revill ♥ 1/3/95 ~ 4/4/96
Aidan Irving Craig ♥ 8/23/96
Aidan Woods ♥ 6/13/80 ~ 7/25/00
Aiden Jones ♥ 4/27/06
Aiden Lee McIver ♥ 12/03/10
Aiden William Thomas ♥ 4/29/09 ~ 2/27/10
Aimee Bird ♥ 8/08/09
Aimee-louise Bates ♥ 10/20/92 ~ 5/16/04
Aishling Marie Roche ♥ 11/18/10 ~ 11/24/10
AJ Markiewicz ♥ 9/5/97 ~ 10/1/97
Aj Timms ♥ 7/12/83 ~ 1/30/06
Akira Mae Gard ♥ 4/11/10 ~ 4/26/10
Alana Boyd-Pollack ♥ 8/4/93 ~ 12/1/11
Alea Grace Frayer ♥ 6/23/06

Aleia Dettmer ♥ 12/7/98 ~ 11/14/10
Aleister Aryan Able Dick ♥ 2/3/11 ~ 3/23/11
Alex "AJ" Owens ♥ 1/3/89 ~ 6/18/13
Alex (Peanut) ♥ 6/30/95 ~ 8/22/12
Alex Daniel Bugenhagen ♥ 3/24/97 ~ 5/31/97
Alex Matheson ♥ 2/17/11 ~ 3/13/11
Alex Simpson ♥ 7/31/07
Alexander F. Farnsworth ♥ 9/5/85 ~ 10/9/10
Alexander Jacob Glant ♥ 10/1/10
Alexander John Whipple ♥ 6/29/09 ~ 4/1/11
Alexander Nicholas Michael Dobbins ♥ 10/1/10 ~ 10/9/10
Alexander Scott Newman ♥ 8/30/11
Alexis Aurora Rave Coleman ♥ 7/4/13 ~ 9/9/13
Alexis Cammile Goudelock ♥ 2/15/07 ~ 4/24/07
Alexis May Harbaugh ♥ 7/8/09 ~ 7/11/10
Alexis Teryn Shaw ♥ 4/12/96 ~ 9/13/09
Alfie James Hone ♥ 11/20/07 ~ 12/28/07
ALia Regina Hughes ♥ 11/13/80 ~ 1/28/13
Alianza Vanessa Garcia ♥ 2/12/94 ~ 6/17/97
Aliza Blay ♥ 6/11/77 ~ 6/10/07
Allison Nicole ♥ 10/99 ~ 6/12
Alton Jess Marshall ♥ 6/3/90 ~ 7/23/09
Alvaro Serna Jr. ♥ 5/24/10
Alyson Bushnell ♥ 1/5/78 ~ 2/20/07
Alyssa Anne Bennett ♥ 12/27/90 ~ 12/24/10
Amanda Brooke Thompson ♥ 2/21/86 ~ 1/30/89
Amanda Elaine Carter ♥ 2/11/88 ~ 4/18/11
Amanda Faith Wooten Forrest ♥ 8/2/03
Amanda Jane Franklin ♥ 1/22/89 ~ 9/26/06
Amanda Louise Clark ♥ 3/19/88 ~ 4/2/07
Amanda Marie Allison ♥ 1/19/93 ~ 1/15/11
Amanda Susan Thierer ♥ 4/28/80 ~ 6/5/07
Amaria Danielle Cook ♥ 9/3/10
Amber Gemma Joyce ♥ 6/16/06
Amber Jean Thompson ♥ 11/15/90 ~ 3/22/09
Amber Lauren (Hays) Vandrey ♥ 1/17/87 ~ 8/16/09
Amber Michelle Kogelis ♥ 4/1/93 ~ 2/25/11
Amber Nicole Davis (Morrison)♥ 1/21/87 ~ 3/8/12
Amelia Louise Keeling ♥ 2/8/08 ~ 3/29/08
Amelia Nancy Field ♥ 9/2/09 ~ 12/21/09

Amiee Marie Luciano ♥ 11/23/91
Amira Justina-Marie Hites ♥ 7/1/10
Amy Louise Turner ♥ 1/31/97 ~ 9/20/09
Analeisa Rose Rivera ♥ 9/21/09 ~ 3/6/11
Andre Jacques Joubert ♥ 7/26/93 ~ 10/4/11
Andre John Archibald ♥ 3/10/11
Andrea Jordan Scherer ♥ 1/30/89~ 1/28/10
Andrew "Andy" John Yeager ♥ 8/74 ~ 4/08
Andrew "Drew" D. Thibodeau ♥ 8/15/78 ~ 9/6/08
Andrew "Yung Pro" Santana ♥ 1/6/93 ~ 10/27/08
Andrew Brinkman ♥ 7/16/90 ~ 7/03/10
Andrew Chard ♥ 2/4/02
Andrew James Black-Matthews ♥ 10/27/06
Andrew James Flick ♥ 12/30/86 ~ 7/8/06
Andrew James Wilson ♥ 12/12/05 ~ 11/07/11
Andrew Justin McPhee ♥ 5/22/97 ~ 12/5/97
Andrew Martin Shoen ♥ 8/23/89 ~ 4/8/11
Andrew Matthew Charles Bransden ♥ 12/20/88 ~ 8/7/10
Andrew Robert John Caul ♥ 4/20/93 ~ 12/8/95
Andrew Scott Wheeler ♥ 9/18/09~10/01/09
Andrew Steven Kellar ♥ 1/20/74 ~ 12/07/93
Andrew Wood ♥ 7/25/74 ~ 12/21/12
Andy Louis Strader III ♥ 8/11/79~ 3/29/80
Angel 2 Morris-Welch ♥ 1/4/06
Angel 3 Morris-Welch ♥ 7/7/06
Angel 4 Morris-Welch ♥ 8/14/07
Angel 5 Morris-Welch ♥ 1/9/10
Angel 6 Morris-Welch ♥ 3/12/10
Angel 7 Morris-Welch ♥ 6/2/11
Angel Anthony Joseph ♥ 12/23/11
Angel Baby Gonzalez-Roldan ♥ 5/2/11
Angel Baby Star ♥ 9/24/05
Angel Baby Twins Fiorino-Baby A♥ 11/14/01;
Baby B ♥ 11/23/01
Angel Chloe Rose Fletcher Parker ♥ 9/11/10~9/11/10
Angel Elaine Craig ♥ 12/19/82 ~ 12/26/82
Angel Gawiuk ♥ 3/16/11
Angel Jack James ♥ 2/14/03
Angel Luis Garcia Jr. ♥ 5/6/75 ~ 8/16/12
Angel Lux Lopez ♥ 6/29/09

Angel Morlok ♥ 5/13/11

Angelica Rae Cartwright ♥ 8/7/95 ~ 6/29/11

Angelina Christine Ramirez. ♥ 8/23/86 ~ 12/13/08

Angelina Lee Escobar ♥ 11/21/89 ~ 9/21/09

Angelito Colula Hernandez ♥ 6/18/10

Angel-Louise Bowers ♥ 11/14/10

Aniyah Hope McKibbin ♥ 8/4/20 ~ 9/12/10

Annie Kate ♥ 6/13/11

Anthony Gee ♥ 8/8/90 ~ 1/28/07

Anthony James Budnack ♥ 3/23/08

Anthony Joseph Mesoraca ♥ 11/01/79~10/03/08

Anthony Joseph Shallo ♥ 2/5/87~10/25/08

Anthony Jr. Richardson ♥ 3/28/89 ~ 8/16/09

Anthony Mason Michael Lancaster ♥ 2/25/74 ~ 9/10/81

Anthony Minutoli ♥ 6/12/92 ~ 7/23/03

Anthony Paul Wodzinski ♥ 1/17/91 ~ 6/10/06

Anthony R. Lamb ♥ 3/9/84 ~ 2/22/10

Anthony Robert Hernandez ♥ 1/14/93 ~ 8/17/09

Anthony Rocco "Rocky" Burton ♥ 3/23/92 ~ 7/05/09

Anthony Victor DeGennaro ♥ 12/2/79 ~ 1/28/97

Anthony Vincent Remshaw ♥ 7/21/75 ~ 7/23/98

April Lynn Brooks ♥ 4/3/96 ~ 5/13/10

April Michelle Pera ♥ 8/2/88~8/7/07

Archie Liam Hopkinson ♥ 7/4/09

Arial Elizbeth Thomas ♥ 12/16/09

Aria-Storm Carey ♥ 6/30/06

Arik Thomas Riddle ♥ 7/29/10

Ashlee Nicole Drouillard ♥ 5/9/95 ~ 11/15/09

Ashlei Rose Walker ♥ 4/11/01 ~ 4/27/01

Ashleigh Anne Love ♥ 9/17/90 ~ 10/6/09

Ashleigh Christine Mauseth ♥ 3/10/92 ~ 9/28/07

Ashleigh Diane Jacobs ♥ 5/3/85 ~ 3/10/12

Ashley Allison Lynch ♥ 2/10/85

Ashley Breann Burchett ♥ 11/9/00 ~ 12/26/00

Ashley Lena Sutton ♥ 8/4/85 ~ 6/7/10

Ashley Marie Martin ♥ 12/16/92 ~ 2/18/13

Ashley Marie O'Kelley ♥ 12/11/96 ~ 11/22/97

Ashley Nicole Stuart ♥ 5/14/89 ~6/25/07

Ashley Remark ♥ 3/8/07 ~ 4/21/07

Ashley Savannah ♥ 7/9/06

Ashlie Duit ♥ 12/21/87 ~ 2/13/09
Ashlyn Breanna Poole ♥ 7/31/90 ~ 1/23/12
Ashton and Kane King ♥ 3/25/08
Aubrey Elaine Cowger ♥ 11/20/89 ~ 3/18/93
Aubrey Skye ♥ 8/22/10
Audrina E Escano ♥ 5/25/91 ~ 12/20/09
Aurora Nicole Pruett ♥ 9/10/09
Austin Clark Zahn ♥ 7/20/06 ~ 7/23/06
Austin James Henry ♥ 11/17/01 ~ 8/22/09
Austin Leonard Launderville ♥ 10/6/90 ~ 2/3/13
Autum Nichole Meeks ♥ 12/18/95~ 2/21/96
Ava and Patrick Scheffler ♥ 6/25/09
Baby Bean ♥ 11/24/06
Baby J. Monzon ♥ 10/20/10
Baby Prince Peter ♥ 2/9/11 ~ 2/13/11
Baker Andrew Troxler ♥ 2/5/11 ~ 4/7/11
Barry Geesey ♥ 4/30/79 ~ 2/18/06
Barry John ♥ 1983 ~ 2009
Baylee Michelle Heblon ♥ 1/30/04 ~ 10/31/04
Benjamin Akira Yatsu ♥ 12/13/95~ 7/10/11
Benjamin Alan Stricklin ♥ 10/3/84 ~ 4/28/00
Benjamin Jarred Chanin ♥ 6/12/94 ~7/26/10
Benjamin Stricklin ♥ 10/3/84 ~ 4/28/00
Bernadette Dawn Ingram ♥ 8/08/84~7/26/09
Blaine Arthur Stoner ♥ 4/13/10
Blake Anthony Callender ♥ 8/14/09 ~ 8/18/09
Blake Easter-Marsh ♥ 12/4/11 ~ 2/13/12
Blake Edward Sobeck ♥ 11/18/84 ~ 11/8/10
Blake Vaughn ♥ 4/21/88 ~ 8/22/13
Bobbie Lynn Wilks ♥ 4/16/88 ~ 10/29/07
Bobby Haight ♥ 10/1/74 ~ 6/16/94
Bobby Shawn Beer ♥ 11/29/82 ~ 3/23/06
Brack Harrison ♥ 12/4/80 ~ 6/13/84
Brad Downs ♥ 7/4/86 ~ 10/6/07
Bradley James Langley ♥ 3/18/91 ~ 4/25/09
Bradley Ryan Place ♥ 8/7/07 ~ 9/14/07
Branden "Bubby" Runion ♥ 6/5/89 ~ 10/20/12
Brandi Lee Hagel ♥ 6/7/76 ~ 2/5/96
Brandi Lynn Mitchell-Edwards. ♥ 2/20/78 ~ 9/17/07
Brandi Lynn Smith ♥ 9/16/83 ~ 7/18/09

Brandon Alan Garcia ♥ 4/24/91~1/5/10
Brandon Austin Letsche ♥ 3/9/95 ~ 8/6/13
Brandon Beckley ♥ 4/21/83~4/14/07
Brandon David Goudie ♥ 6/2/05 ~ 8/17/10
Brandon Dewayne Martin ♥ 12/16/92 ~ 8/2/08
Brandon James Higgins ♥ 9/19/89 ~ 3/20/13
Brandon Lee Bricker ♥ 1/15/97 ~ 7/10/06
Brandon Lee McGlothlin ♥ 12/31/88 ~ 5/21/11
Brandon Lee McWilliams ♥ 6/17/93 ~4/30/10
Brandon Matthew Goodpaster ♥ 5/14/94 ~ 9/8/10
Brandon Michael Whitby ♥ 1/22/86~08/21/08
Brandon Mitchell Harrison-Douglas ♥ 6/3/94 ~ 2/18/06
Brandon Phillip Talbert ♥ 3/26/92 ~ 4/8/11
Brandon Robert Harris ♥ 11/14/04 ~ 12/11/11
Brandon Tyler Beshada ♥ 3/21/1982 ~ 4/1/07
Brandon Wade Barnett ♥ 1/28/10
Brayden Russell Zieg ♥ 1/5/07 ~ 6/6/08
Breanne and Brennae Harjo ♥ 6/6/08
Brendan Samuel Ward ♥ 9/26/01 ~ 9/27/01
Brenden Louis Lowenberg ♥ 3/9/85 ~ 2/15/12
Brenden Reese Spring ♥ 2/22/92
Brett Randall Jaynes ♥ 12/24/88~5/24/11
Brian "BeeKay" Kerr ♥ 2/3/92 ~ 3/26/11
Brian "Bubba" Paul Bowling ♥ 5/01/81 ~ 10/19/96
Brian Andrew Wentworth ♥ 1/10/95 ~ 3/6/10
Brian Balzer ♥ 12/9/86 ~ 10/29/09
Brian Charles Ernst ♥ 3/11/91 ~ 3/16/10
Brian Edward Clark ♥ 9/20/90 ~ 6/21/08
Brian Eldridge ♥ 5/14/80 ~ 9/5/13
Brian Eric ♥ 10/6/69 ~ 12/21/12
Brian Frederick Perrault ♥ 8/27/93 ~ 12/1/06
Briana Becerra ♥ 3/18/02 ~ 1/26/10
Brianna Allen ♥ 12/11/99 ~ 5/22/00
Brianna Emily Silliker ♥ 1/4/94 ~ 11/4/10
Brianna Renee Rogers ♥ 12/11/99 ~ 5/22/00
Brice Connel Parsons ♥ 3/20/11 ~ 3/27/11
Brigit Elizabeth McGee ♥ 10/24/00 ~ 10/26/00
Britni Nicole Jaynes ♥ 5/8/87~11/26/87
Brittany M. Jenkins ♥ 8/26/94 ~ 1/20/03
Brittany Nicole Thomas ♥ 3/12/88 ~2/27/10

Brooke Gemma Mayon ♥ 6/18/09
Brooke Sierra Fleming ♥ 2/26/01
Brooklyn Gladun ♥ 6/7/11
Bryan Christopher Plunkett ♥ 1/12/85 ~ 10/28/02
Bryan Keith Gamble ♥ 5/18/97 ~ 5/22/97
Byron Mallett ♥ 2/10/00 ~ 8/22/13
Byron Reid Clink ♥ 8/17/10
Cade James Bailey ♥ 10/17/00 ~ 9/21/10
Caden Jorden Ansin ♥ 10/03/06 ~ 2/23/11
Cailou Boswell ♥ 4/8/10
Caleb Burne King ♥ 4/6/11
Caleb Michael Wiesen ♥ 6/1/11
Callum John Gorton ♥ 4/21/09 ~ 8/7/09
Cameron Robert Wolfe ♥ 11/5/04
Camillie M. White ♥ 3/7/04 ~ 6/25/04
Camryn Lee Shultz ♥ 10/29/11 ~ 10/27/13
Candice Hynes ♥ 8/26/98
Cara Marie Holley ♥ 8/19/91 ~ 7/7/10
Carl Joathon Lambert ♥ 3/12/82 ~ 1/23/02
Carliser M Rodriquez ♥ 11/27/74 ~ 1/31/10
Carston Wayne Kownack ♥ 11/17/03 ~ 8/1/08
Casey Alexander Stricker ♥ 12/18/01 ~ 9/24/11
Casey Beals ♥ 4/13/90 ~ 1/18/13
Casey Faye Marie Aschan-Cox ♥ 4/8/92 ~ 3/18/10
Casey Luffman ♥ 2/27/90 ~ 4/6/09
Casey Michele Costello ♥ 7/25/91 ~ 9/21/91
Casey Nicole Pannochia ♥ 6/10/89 ~3/23/09
Cassandra Baker ♥ 4/5/85 ~ 8/10/08
Cassandra Goeddel ♥ 4/24/82 ~ 8/15/13
Cassidy Joy Andel ♥ 10/26/94 ~ 11/4/10
Cassie Elizabeth Myers ♥ 12/23/97 ~ 9/30/02
Cayden Wince ♥ 12/12/94 ~ 1/31/07
Cayleb Ralph-Joseph ♥ 8/1/00
Cayliss Treahn Mothershed ♥ 12/1/93 ~ 11/14/11
Cecilia Kay Balma ♥ 1/5/06 ~ 4/7/09
Cerridwyn "Kerry" Maire Ursula Brigid Roseanne Lujan ♥
5/17/89 ~ 5/20/08
Chad Michael, Madison Marie and Bailey Jean Horton ♥ 9/11/09
Chanel Peckham. ♥ 6/30/08 ~ 4/6/10
Chaos David-Michael Hotes ♥ 1/12/11
Charlene Ashley Maloney ♥ 7/11/92 ~ 5/16/12

Charlene Whitethread ♥ 5/26/81
Charles Alan Williams ♥ 8/7/90 ~ 12/17/09
Charles Daniel Hillhouse ♥ 8/28/86 ~ 8/28/08
Charles Patrick Mottram ♥ 1/18/88~7/13/10
Charles Vincent Michael Agricola ♥ 4/14/89 ~ 10/19/07
Charlie Jack Grady ♥ 3/27/10
Charlie Kelly ♥ 3/16/70 ~ 7/11/99
Charlotte Elise Walker ♥ 3/14/98 ~ 2/20/08
Chase Cameron Cummings ♥ 10/9/93 ~ 9/18/12
Chase Christopher Wright ♥ 7/10/10
Chaun Dale Lambert ♥ 7/11/76 ~ 9/21/00
Chelsea Ann Morgan ♥ 3/16/94
Chelsea Lynn Munson ♥ 1/18/90 ~ 2/11/12
Chelsea R. Murphy ♥ 3/18/92 ~ 3/4/08
Chene Engelbrecht ♥ 3/11/87 ~ 10/7/91
Cheyanne Karen Audet ♥ 10/13/80 ~ 10/27/11
Cheyenne Anjelica Decker (Jackson) ♥ 11/19/94
Cheyenne Haines ♥ 9/26/86 ~ 4/27/10
Chris Gerlt Jr. ♥ 8/78 ~ 11/98
Chriss Therron Smith ♥ 4/18/74
Chrissy Emmons ♥ 5/6/85 ~ 1/17/10
Christian Cade Lowery ♥ 1/4/97 ~ 9/15/08
Christian Frechette ♥ 10/17/02 ~ 7/13/07
Christian Sain Livingston ♥ 8/9/10
Christian Sean Jorgensen ♥ 12/9/77 ~ 1/18/10
Christian Taelor and Austyn Shane ♥ 4/11/98
Christian Webb ♥ 11/30/08 ~ 12/2/08
Christina Marie Smith ♥ 5/15/87 ~ 2/6/12
Christina Stellato ♥ 10/14/80 ~ 8/17/10
Christopher "Chit" Amedee ♥ 11/4/93 ~ 2/19/09
Christopher "Chris" L. Stiles. ♥ 1/18/84 ~ 6/20/10
Christopher "CJ" John Wheatley ♥ 1/26/85 ~ 1/1/10
Christopher "Critter" Joseph Smith ♥ 12/11/97 ~ 4/21/11
Christopher Allen Reinhardt ♥ 10/4/08 ~ 10/3/07
Christopher Bolduc ♥ 8/20/90 ~ 7/23/02
Christopher Bynum Younts ♥ 8/7/03 ~ 12/20/03
Christopher Charles "Charlie" Gordon ♥ 12/13/00 ~ 12/7/09
Christopher Collins ♥ 4/19/75
Christopher Dafoe ♥ 11/15/82 ~ 10/6/07
Christopher E. (Burger) Barski ♥ 10/30/78 ~ 3/25/13

Christopher Josef Locke ♥ 11/7/06 ~ 12/17/06
Christopher Karamitros ♥ 1/13/82 ~ 1/6/10
Christopher Kessler ♥ 6/16/78
Christopher Proctor ♥ 12/29/81 ~ 5/13/98
Christopher R.Garner ♥ 8/17/90 ~ 4/12/92
Christopher Robert Swartz ♥ 7/11/80 ~ 8/29/10
Christopher Sansome ♥ 8/19/69~8/29/69
Christopher Shane Jones ♥ 6/14/89 ~ 9/3/89
Christopher Wayne Heath ♥ 6/10/88 ~ 12/10/09
Cian JonRichard McCorkle ♥ 11/14/07 ~ 11/28/09
Claire Elizabeth Stroud ♥ 10/26/11
Clay Ellis ♥ 6/13/93 ~ 8/23/94
Clint Wheatley ♥ 6/9/78 ~ 8/27/02
Clinton Terry Milam ♥ 4/07/93 ~ 8/05/03
Cody Adam Acton ♥ 5/18/90 ~ 10/16/10
Cody Dean Field ♥ 3/16/95 ~ 7/3/95
Cody Michael Green ♥ 1/22/89 ~ 2/9/09
Cody Ray Scarbrough ♥ 7/2/02 ~ 4/28/09
Cole Chandler Gray ♥ 10/5/05
Colin Matthew Scott Ingham ♥ 12/14/09 ~ 12/28/09
Colin Michael "Mike" Ewers ♥ 12/18/81 ~ 6/21/03
Colleen Marie Douglass ♥ 5/12/61 ~ 5/18/92
Collin Xavier Coloura ♥ 4/18/11
Collins Randall Huffman ♥ 5/18/11 ~ 5/19/11
Colton Hunter Perry Hopkins ♥ 5/7/99 ~ 12/5/04
Conner and Kennedy ♥ 7/24/09
Connor James and Collin Michael Conklin ♥ 10/14/10
Conor Nelson Tye ♥ 12/76 ~ 6/09
Cooper Douglas Stulz ♥ 10/15/01 ~ 4/13/10
Cooper John Mayon ♥ 4/20/07
Corey Andrew Evans ♥ 10/1/87 ~ 11/19/09
Corey Christopher Goad ♥ 8/13/87
Corrinna Marie Romero ♥ 7/3/73 ~ 5/21/04
Courtney "Blondie" Ann Koehler ♥ 5/24/94 ~ 8/16/07
Courtney "Boo" Rae Miller ♥ 9/17/97 ~ 11/13/10
Courtney Jane Houldey ♥ 8/10/01
Craig G. Lewtas ♥ 10/7/70 ~ 7/28/09
Craig Michael Copsey ♥ 6/02/80 ~ 10/08/08
Craig R. Bresson ♥ 1/08/85 ~ 11/26/06
Craig Steven Doubt III ♥ 9/30/89 ~ 9/8/08

Crawford Alan Carnahan ♥ 8/21/88 ~ 5/12/07
Crystal Mae Lopez ♥ 11/18/76 ~ 11/20/09
Curt B. Allred Jr. ♥ 6/26/76 ~ 1/16/09
Curtis Charles Lewis ♥ 5/26/70 ~ 6/20/06
Daisha Rosemary Rogers ♥ 4/5/94 ~ 11/27/94
Dakota Shane Casey ♥ 12/31/91 ~ 1/12/92
Dakota Wayne Hoffman-Bennett ♥ 2/23/02 ~ 1/29/11
Dakotah Rayne Dougherty ♥ 7/7/99 ~ 9/6/99
Dallas Orion Caswell-Snyder ♥ 1/1/05
Dalton Lee Davis ♥ 11/2/56 ~1/22/89
Dameon S. Norman ♥ 12/17/70 ~ 4/12/06
Damian John Richardson ♥ 10/31/83 ~ 11/15/02
Damian Kent ♥ 10/28/92 ~ 11/27/10
Damien Joseph Brian Hordell ♥ 12/9/07 ~ 4/22/08
Damien Michael Gorse ♥ 10/20/01 ~ 11/6/01
Damir Geovanny Baker ♥ 7/16/11
Dan Kelley ♥ 6/18/75 ~ 10/2/08
Dana Richard Cackowski ♥ 9/18/84 ~ 10/2/09
Daniel Anthony Patterson ♥ 4/9/95 ~ 3/10/98
Daniel Aust ♥ 7/7/76 ~ 8/9/03
Daniel Clark Gale ♥ 5/5/94 ~ 3/8/10
Daniel J Martinez ♥ 8/7/77 ~ 7/5/11
Daniel Jadon Pruett ♥ 12/12/04
Daniel James Amar ♥ 10/08/85 ~ 7/24/97
Daniel Joseph Whisler ♥ 12/11/70 ~ 6/27/09
Daniel Matthew Imhoff ♥ 6/11/88 ~ 12/18/10
Daniel N. Krehbiel ♥ 5/6/96 ~ 11/28/08
Daniel P. Kelley ♥ 6/18/75 ~ 10/2/08
Daniel Ronk ♥ 3/15/91 ~ 4/7/10
Daniel Steven ♥ 1/02/11
Daniel Tanner Gehrman ♥ 3/2/13 ~ 3/2/13
Daniel Walsh ♥ 11/8/83 ~ 7/15/02
Daniel-Alexander ♥ 2/15/97 ~ 7/25/74
Danielle Louise Keelan ♥ 7/11/90 ~ 8/31/09
Danielle N. Trevithick. ♥ 6/28/88 ~ 8/12/10
Danielle Pauline Murphy ♥ 5/26/81 ~ 1/29/06
Danny Bo Mei ♥ 5/17/10
Danny DeSantis Jr. ♥ 8/07/67 ~ 9/10/05
Danny James Gominsky ♥ 8/12/58 ~ 2/20/12
Danny Watson Jr. ♥ 8/16/73 ~ 4/25/04

Dante Avery Nathaniel Milford ♥ 8/27/97 ~ 11/12/97
Darien M. Wilson ♥ 4/29/83 ~ 1/4/06
Daris J. Shields ♥ 11/28/80 ~ 11/03/10
Darren Grant ♥ 3/31/73 ~ 12/21/07
Darren Junior Marsh ♥ 2/13/06 ~ 5/5/06
Darren Marsh ♥ 9/6/83 ~ 10/28/05
Dauson Alijah Bim Peace ♥ 2/24/05 ~ 5/26/06
David August Cardenas ♥ 7/7/98 ~ 11/10/10
David Duanne Rouse ♥ 7/10/88 ~ 8/20/08
David Dustin Finch ♥ 11/30/86 ~ 12/8/10
David Edward Maclay ♥ 11/26/03 ~ 7/19/11
David Jay Kestner ♥ 5/14/93
David Jordan Bachner ♥ 1/16/91 ~ 8/11/09
David Mark Vitiello Jr. ♥ 3/27/89 ~ 11/06/08
David Michael Russell ♥ 7/23/02
David Thomas Snow ♥ 6/15/09
Dawn M. (Paul) Reynolds ♥ 1/14/74 ~ 12/08/09
Dawn Marie Miller ♥ 6/9/70 ~ 10/22/92
Debbie Unruh ♥ 5/30/85 ~ 8/7/07
Debbie V. Kern ♥ 10/17/70 ~ 1/25/92
DebbieAnn Palmeri ♥ 3/10/85 ~ 3/14/85
Dennis Anthony Farr ♥ 2/9/87 ~ 3/6/11
Denver Ray Stubrich ♥ 7/14/97
Derek Christopher Mackay ♥ 8/5/87 ~ 9/15/08
Derrick Bradley Stubrich ♥ 7/22/83 ~ 3/10/13
Destiny Ann-Maureen Chesebro ♥ 5/3/11
Destiny Marie Cissell ♥ 5/4/99 ~ 10/27/09
Devan Christopher White ♥ 5/11/95 ~ 1/7/11
Devin Jacob McKibbin ♥ 7/28/09
Devin Taylor Johnson ♥ 7/22/91 ~ 11/5/10
Devon Daniel Morrison ♥ 11/1/02 ~ 9/14/13
Devon James Kushman ♥ 10/27/04
Dillon Ray Jett ♥ 1/15/87 ~ 5/09/10
Dino Valentino Raponi ♥ 6/2/77 ~ 1/20/07
Dominick Jason Barajas ♥ 12/19/92 ~ 12/19/10
Dominik Luke Pinzone ♥ 4/03/85 ~ 12/13/05
Don Glen Thornhill ♥ 5/6/93 ~ 8/22/09
Donald W. Craig ♥ 1/8/35 ~ 2/8/82
Donaway Shylow Rego ♥ 5/23/88 ~ 10/24/09
Dorothy Dawn Palmer ♥ 3/14/91 ~ 11/3/07

Doug Hess ♥ 1/12/96 ~ 7/28/13
Dustin Koby Wunderlich ♥ 4/19/84 ~ 3/13/13
Dustin L. Hooten ♥ 7/1/84 ~ 10/14/02
Dustin Lovett ♥ 6/15/81 ~ 4/7/05
Dustin Ross Murphy ♥ 9/24/85 ~ 4/15/10
Dustin Wayne Plyler ♥ 11/27/03
Dylan and Evan Lima Pechilis ♥ 7/19/07
Dylan James George ♥ 11/8/91 ~ 9/2/12
Dylan Kirby Montgomery ♥ 2/24/10 ~ 2/24/10
Dylan Markwell ♥ 12/19/05 ~ 12/24/05
Dylan Patrick Major ♥ 12/4/81 ~ 12/4/81
Eddie Porrazzo ♥ 10/31/71 ~ 1/15/10
Edmund Thomas Roland ♥ 7/10/86 ~ 7/10/07
Eduardo "Eddy" Jorge Triana ♥ 5/15/75 ~ 4/13/11
Eilidh Beth Simpson ♥ 9/24/10
Elias Michael Cole ♥ 9/30/08 ~ 10/15/08
Elijah "Eli" Xavier Elmore ♥ 10/7/10 ~ 12/14/10
Elijah Manuel Eilets ♥ 6/10/03
Elijah Seth Moye ♥ 12/15/81 ~ 1/5/01
Elijah Zaine Caro Cooper ♥ 5/11/01 ~ 10/12/08
Elin Marianne Ossiander ♥ 6/3/10
Elisa Mendez ♥ 3/10/83 ~ 8/13/12
Elisabeth Evelyn Allread ♥ 8/11/83 ~ 8/24/08
Elizabeth Hudson ♥ 5/20/87 ~ 4/11/08
Elizabeth Paige Cornes ♥ 8/14/96 ~ 2/25/07
Ellen Rose Floyd (McGuiggan) ♥ 8/23/92 ~ 4/4/10
Elliana Alyssa Zaidel ♥ 7/18/05 ~ 7/13/07
Ellie Brooke Wilkinson ♥ 3/5/07 ~ 1/25/11
Emilee Skye and Dylen Jacob Hummel ♥ 11/18/11
Emily & Emilio Garcia ♥ 2/25/93
Emily Lynn Brown and unborn child ♥ 8/8/82 ~ 1/15/09
Emily Mae Martin ♥ 9/19/00 ~ 7/16/01
Emily Rose Ford ♥ 9/28/10 ~ 10/10/10
Emma Christine Thomas ♥ 4/10/08 ~ 9/18/09
Emma Frances Dalton ♥ 9/22/10 ~ 4/17/11
Emma Louise Jessop ♥ 12/31/87 ~ 8/29/10
Emma Stephens Armstrong ♥ 2/12/09 ~ 2/15/10
Enrique "Ricky" Lopez, Jr ♥ 1/12/89 ~ 7/30/10
Ephraim David Schultz ♥ 7/19/83 ~ 5/12/05
Eric Anthony Dyke ♥ 3/30/81 ~ 11/4/06

Eric Hargrave ♥ 8/17/83 ~ 11/04/08
Eric John Simco ♥ 10/4/81 ~ 7/28/08
Eric Nicholas Irby ♥ 5/28/87 ~ 5/4/11
Eric Partin ♥ 1/20/87 ~ 5/30/10
Eric Ronald Schwed ♥ 9/6/87 ~ 9/8/97
Eric Ryan Dudley ♥ 10/12/1984 ~ 11/05/11
Erica Sellers ♥ 5/5/90 ~ 8/9/09
Erika Joy Rowan ♥ 9/23/91 ~ 2/25/08
Erika Kelly Anstett ♥ 3/12/82 ~ 2/18/03
Ernest Richard Farris ♥ 10/8/92
Ernesto Rojo Jr. ♥ 10/21/11 ~ 8/14/13
Ethan Carter Lane ♥ 3/12/10 ~ 6/4/10
Ethan Cody Bleu Saltar ♥ 12/15/93 ~ 9/19/10
Evelyn Cheryl Chadwick-Sawyer ♥ 3/17/11
Faith Fogarty ♥ 10/13/99
Felipe Catalan ♥ 8/24/85 ~ 10/28/06
Feodora Laurent Kushman ♥10/31/08
Finlay John Houlding ♥ 9/5/10
Franchesca Mercedese Rowell ♥ 3/3/97
Frankie Aaron Gallimore ♥ 7/25/88 ~ 10/8/08
Freddie Endres ♥ 8/05/97 ~ 8/02/10
Gabriel Lopez ♥ 7/23/81 ~ 7/23/05
Gage Scott Williams ♥ 8/4/10
Garrett James Smith ♥ 9/24/92 ~ 5/15/10
Gavin Matthew King ♥ 6/3/87 ~ 8/14/09
Gemma Keely Mayon ♥ 1/11/08
Genoveva Soriano Salazar ♥ 9/22/57 ~ 11/12/82
Geoffrey P. Edwards ♥ 5/6/84 ~ 5/22/02
George Patrick Joseph Gamblin III ♥ 1/28/84 ~ 7/26/10
George-Paul Webb ♥ 4/10/92
Georgia Elise Douglass ♥ 5/2/02 ~ 1/21/05
Gerrit Storm ♥ 7/9/91 ~ 11/28/98
Gian Leo A. Combalicer ♥ 10/6/13 ~ 10/11/13
Grace Samantha Mayri Hilbert. ♥ 3/17/11
Gracie Stultz ♥ 1/27/10
Gracie-Rose Lane ♥ 12/6/10 ~ 12/6/10
Gregory Edward Whale Jr. ♥ 9/2/91 ~ 4/26/10
Gunnar Hosia Dougherty ♥ 4/27/98
Hailey Nevaeh'Lea Stolz ♥ 4/28/06 ~ 8/22/06
Hailey Nicole Larsen ♥ 12/23/08 ~ 7/28/10

Hannah Gerlt ♥ 7/3/03 ~ 7/17/10
Harley Davidson Bivens ♥ 7/15/87 ~ 6/19/05
Harley Jay Fox ♥ 4/25/01 ~ 6/10/08
Harlow Elizabeth Schaefer ♥ 5/21/11 ~ 6/15/11
Harold W. Smith, Jr. ♥ 5/23/74 ~ 3/28/10
Harvey Dylan Merchant ♥ 9/7/07
Hayden Allen Kimbell ♥ 3/20/10
Hayden Andrew ♥ 1/17/04
Hayley Patricia Aird ♥ 6/24/10 ~ 6/28/10
Heather Brookshire ♥ 4/13/81 ~ 5/21/08
Heather Corinn Schwartz ♥ 10/12/90 ~ 10/28/09
Heather Lynn Russell ♥ 7/28/79 ~ 5/4/09
Heidi Lynn Crawford ♥ 8/18/89
Henry William Berlin ♥ 2/23/06 ~ 7/22/08
Hollie Michelle Battershill ♥ 4/21/01
Hope Elna Lockhart ♥ 11/19/10
Hubert George Rose 4th ♥ 12/19/78 ~ 7/15/12
Hunnie Beth Lance ♥ 12/26/79 ~ 10/8/09
Ian James Foster ♥ 11/10/77 ~ 9/8/06
Ian Thomas Kosky ♥ 6/11/80 ~ 10/15/10
Ieisha Pipon Doreen Coulineur ♥ 1/10/98 ~ 4/21/11
Isaac Marvin-Lee Stokes ♥ 2/12/03
Isabel Martins ♥ 7/25/97 ~ 3/10/11
Isabel Simone Fiorino ♥ 5/2/03 ~ 12/17/05
Isabella Faith Karol ♥ 8/23/11
Isabella Marie Crispino ♥ 1/12/10
Isabella Maybre Kinard ♥ 12/26/10
Isaiah M. Alonso ♥ 4/26/04 ~ 9/10/10
Isaiah Matthew Mangum ♥ 10/22/98
Ishmal-joshua Thomas ♥ 12/4/04
Itty and Bitty Lux Lopez ♥ 6/22/01
Izaya Michael Baiz ♥ 8/12/03 ~ 11/27/08
J. Grant Lewis ♥ 12/19/79 ~ 1/17/06
J. Michael Brooksher ♥ 8/19/89 ~ 12/12/11
Jack Greg Reynolds-McCourt ♥ 7/23/10
Jack James Dickey ♥ 4/7/98 ~ 6/15/06
Jack L. Garner ♥ 12/13/67 ~ 11/18/11
Jackilynn Rainn Stoermer ♥ 5/15/04 ~ 6/6/04
Jacklyn Christine Hoover ♥ 1/20/92 ~ 8/28/11
Jacob "Jake" Alexander-Lee Gagnon ♥ 5/1/03 ~ 9/25/08

Jacob "Jake" Anthony Perez ♥ 7/20/98 ~ 12/17/09
Jacob Kyle Johnson ♥ 11/19/83 ~ 11/26/97
Jacob Laurence Geiser ♥ 5/17/06 ~ 1/15/08
Jacob Michael Scott McLeod-Steinmetz ♥ 6/17/91 ~ 6/16/05
Jacob Ryan Yergeau ♥ 9/25/99 ~ 9/25/99
Jacob Michael Nelson ♥ 10/18/08 ~ 5/20/12
Jade BoRam Mebane ♥ 9/24/95 ~ 3/22/12
Jadra Hawkins ♥ 1/9/09
Jaiden John Page ♥ 2/4/11
Jaime Patton Daugherty ♥ 10/1/09
Jaise Michael Taylor 'Bear' ♥ 8/3/08 ~ 9/29/10
Jakylar Leon Burns ♥ 10/5/08 ~ 2/2/11
Jamal Thomas "Tommy" EL-Ferkh ♥ 5/8/08
James "Jamie" W. McCombs Jr. ♥ 2/12/73 ~ 5/12/98.
James "Jay" Heath Jr. ♥ 10/7/87 ~ 3/8/09
James Amato Jr. ♥ 1/10/86 ~ 10/03/10
James Brandon Smith ♥ 1/18/80 ~ 7/29/02
James Jeffrey Burnette ♥ 1/14/76 ~ 6/18/08
James L. Peterson ♥ 4/6/80 ~ 3/19/07
James L. Vandewater IV ♥ 1/28/86 ~ 11/3/07
James Melford Young III ♥ 1/29/91 ~ 8/6/09
James Raymond Knowles ♥ 12/1/88 ~ 3/25/89
James Reid Clink ♥ 8/17/10
James Thomas Castaneda ♥ 10/2/08
James Thomas Galanti-Smith ♥ 2/23/10
James Thomas Grose ♥ 3/9/76 ~ 12/27/07
James Thomas Price ♥ 3/24/96 ~ 11/1/96
Jamie Lyons ♥ 2/23/90 ~ 2/25/90
Jarod Alan Scott ♥ 3/23/81 ~ 9/19/09
Jaron Keith Morgan ♥ 8/31/89 ~6/27/12
Jason C. Cooper ♥ 9/21/78 ~ 4/30/04
Jason Christopher Moore ♥ 5/24/72 ~ 3/17/11
Jason Daniello ♥ 9/26/97 ~ 7/24/11
Jason Frank Meyers ♥ 3/18/85 ~ 3/22/09
Jason Gray Thompson ♥ 8/24/80 ~ 10/13/07
Jason James Olinger ♥ 4/20/71 ~ 12/17/11
Jason Lee Webb ♥ 3/28/76 ~ 9/21/92
Jason M. Burke ♥ 5/5/75 ~ 11/30/01
Jason Patrick N.Infante ♥ 7/2/94 ~ 8/12/12
Jason Phillip Brooks ♥ 10/18/84 ~ 8/8/10

Jason Ray Peyton ♥ 11/01/94 ~ 4/28/11
Jason Robert Maddox ♥ 11/17/09 ~ 11/22/09
Jaxson Benjamin Norton ♥ 10/31/06 ~ 3/30/11
Jay Garrison ♥ 10/93
Jayden Blake Schneider ♥ 1/15/11
Jaydin Lamont ♥ 10/18/03
Jayjay Howard Donovan ♥ 4/06/09
Jaylib JaQai Butler ♥ 5/9/05 ~ 9/28/05
Jaz'myn Marie Buress ♥ 8/18/13 ~ 10/8/13
Jeff King ♥ 9/18/74 ~ 3/11/11
Jeffrey Call ♥ 8/9/99~1/17/11
Jeffrey T. Felix ♥ 11/30/72 ~ 1/29/99
Jema Michelle Harjo ♥ 4/12/09
Jennifer Alyson Bushnell ♥ 1/5/78 ~ 2/20/07.
Jennifer Ann Greenwald ♥ 10/24/81 ~ 3/16/98
Jennifer E. Chaffin-Kinnee ♥ 9/14/73 ~ 1/14/13
Jennifer Jane Metcalfe ♥ 11/6/85 ~ 2/8/10
Jennifer Lynn Rider ♥ 4/28/86 ~ 8/24/12
Jennifer Michelle Banks ♥ 6/4/76 ~ 7/27/00
Jenny Lynn Morris ♥ 5/4/79 ♥ 12/4/96
Jeremiah Isaac Deskins ♥ 9/21/07~1/12/08
Jeremy "Worm" Lawson ♥ 5/3/86 ~ 2/14/10
Jeremy Andrew Barnes ♥ 11/23/80 ~ 9/8/98
Jeremy Austin Wagner ♥ 8/18/00 ~ 9/5/00
Jeremy Jayson Marshall ♥ 4/26/75 ~ 9/10/01
Jeremy Lee Ward ♥ 12/31/86 ~ 3/23/09
Jeremy Lynn Alcorn ♥ 11/8/86 ~ 6/15/09
Jeremy Paul Karrer ♥ 1/25/80 ~ 1/7/87
Jeremy Reece Foote ♥ 8/14/88 ~ 1/27/10
Jeremy Robert Smith ♥ 11/21/71 ~ 5/31/10
Jermey Dee Gill ♥ 6/8/83 ~ 10/25/05
Jerry "Junior" Stevens II ♥ 8/7/91 ~ 7/18/09
Jerry Darren Austin ♥ 12/29/82 ~ 4/16/83
Jerry Torres ♥ 2/7/85 ~ 11/14/03
Jesse B Gatts ♥ 5/16/95 ~ 3/30/11
Jesse James McEathron ♥ 9/13/90 ~ 3/18/09
Jesse Lockamy ♥ 4/18/83 ~ 11/17/99
Jesse Voinski ♥ 2/23/80 ~ 5/12/08
Jessica Danielle Herrington ♥ 1/15/92 ~ 1/20/09
Jessica Goreham ♥ 6/23/06

Jessica Grenier ♥ 5/31/83 ~ 1/22/11
Jessica Kate Willrich ♥ 2/6/82 ~ 8/28/06
Jessica Marie Gleason ♥ 3/7/82 ~ 2/22/05
Jessica Pirkel ♥ 6/16/85 ~ 6/19/87
Jesus Guadalupe Rios ♥ 6/5/13
Jethro James ♥ 3/10/11 ~ 3/10/11
Jill Marie Gregory ♥ 3/16/73 ~ 8/14/08
Jimma Gabrelle Cape-Kiser ♥ 6/16/02 ~ 9/19/09
Jimmie Andrew Hawkins ♥ 4/7/84 ~ 10/6/11
Joe Elliot ♥ 8/13/99
Joe Keel ♥ 6/1/80 ~ 4/10/13
Joe King ♥ 7/3/63 ~ 11/18/05
Joey Scarpa ♥ 9/13/71 ~ 3/20/95
John Andrew Hall ♥ 10/6/71 ~ 7/1/10
John Edward Pegan IV ♥ 7/29/10 ~ 8/20/10
John Jacob Thomas Richey ♥ 4/3/88 ~ 6/19/05
John Michael Delehanty ♥ 1/25/88 ~ 11/1/08
John Michael McConnell ♥ 3/23/10 ~ 4/30/10
John Paul Hughes ♥ 10/3/89 ~ 8/7/07
John Paul Smith ♥ 3/20/95 ~ 12/14/04
John Tartagia Jr. ♥ 11/22/82 ~ 8/13/05
John Travis Gordon ♥ 2/11/73 ~ 5/18/08
John Wayne Corcoran ♥ 7/10/98 ~ 10/9/09
Johnathan M. Burns ♥ 1/8/83 ~ 11/17/00
John-Benjamin Bohannon ♥ 4/7/87 ~ 12/24/08
Johnna Giordano ♥ 2/12/93 ~ 12/24/10
Johnnie Derden ♥ 11/17/66 ~ 10/2/04
Johnny Bob Moore ♥ 10/4/71 ~ 9/18/13
Johnny Eddy Potter ♥ 12/12/06 ~ 12/14/06
Jonah Alexander Cullett ♥ 2/24/94 ~ 5/23/10
Jonah Chen Glovsky ♥ 12/16/96 ~ 12/20/96
Jonathan Alexander Hancock ♥ 12/19/75 ~ 4/9/95
Jonathan Hall ♥ 5/2/83 ~ 12/23/10 and
Grandson ♥ 10/15/09 ~ 1/10/10
Jonathan Hunter Helwig ♥ 1/26/90 ~ 12/27/10
Jonathan Murillo Lopez ♥ 8/30/00 ~ 11/27/00
Jonathan T. Kormondy (J5) ♥ 3/17/71 ~ 12/10/10
Jonathan Wade Virden ♥ 5/4/89 ~ 10/4/12
Jonathen Brent Byrom ♥ 4/4/90 ~ 11/31/92
Jordan "Jordy" Walsh ♥ 1/14/98 ~ 3/2/07

Jordan Alexander Gallo ♥ 4/30/86
Jordan Avery Killian ♥ 11/19/93 ~ 8/13/07
Jordan Edward "Boomer" Mountjoy ♥ 4/21/90 ~ 4/30/07
Jordan Gregory Darrell ♥ 5/14/04 ~ 7/23/13
Jordan John Gose ♥ 6/15/87 ~ 6/12/10
Jordan Michael King ♥ 10/1/90 ~ 1/4/10
Jordan Paul Hacker ♥ 1/2/88 ~ 12/7/09
Jordan Sammy Rutherford ♥ 2/24/11
Jordyn M. Vaughn ♥ 10/13/99 ~ 6/25/04
Jose' Alfredo Colula Hernandez ♥ 7/28/09
Joseph "Joey" Anthony Gordon ♥ 11/22/81~ 6/19/02
Joseph Andrew Armstead ♥ 4/9/01 ~ 1/2/10
Joseph Anthony Scalise ♥ 11/02/90 ~ 6/22/09
Joseph Conner Weeks ♥ 9/22/93 ~ 10/16/13
Joseph Heverin ♥ 4/08/85 ~ 2/25/08
Joseph Michael Alkema ♥ 1/6/11 ~ 5/13/11
Joseph Paul King ♥ 11/29/87 ~ 3/26/10
Joseph Ryan Marino ♥ 9/6/93 ~ 8/13/09
Joseph Sewayah Ward ♥ 9/26/01
Joseph Tracy Baptista ♥ 10/18/99 ~ 3/30/07
Josephine "Josie" Francisco Herrera ♥ 9/1/91 ~ 10/13/10
Joshua " Boo Boo" Gage Pierson ♥ 9/28/08 ~ 4/29/10
Joshua "Dean" Hill ♥ 10/12/90 ~ 11/30/09
Joshua Angel Echelbarger ♥ 3/30/10 ~ 3/31/10
Joshua David Maitland ♥ 4/10/91 ~ 5/31/91
Joshua Eric Harrison ♥ 2/22/83 ~ 9/30/09
Joshua James Villatoro ♥ 12/18/10 ~ 3/27/11
Joshua Jay Farrar ♥ 3/13/82 ~ 3/11/04
Joshua Michael Barnfield ♥ 11/23/89 ~ 8/25/11
Joshua Paul Cope ♥ 7/25/79 ~ 8/12/00
Joshua Tyler Podsobinskin ♥ 3/21/93
Joshuajames M. Korczykowski ♥ 9/21/83 ~ 4/8/10
Julian Balboa ♥ 1/15/93 ~ 11/4/99
Julie Heather Hope Hall ♥ 2/20/76
July Marie Barrick ♥ 7/12/94 ~ 5/4/10
Justin Bice ♥ 9/16/88 ~ 3/8/08
Justin D. Burkhart ♥ 5/02/81 ~ 8/01/09
Justin Ellis Tidwell ♥ 10/8/91 ~ 7/20/09
Justin Fredrick Mitchell ♥ 6/30/82 ~ 3/21/07
Justin Hayes Wilson ♥ 8/8/01 ~ 5/21/10

Justin Jeffries ♥ 3/17/90 ~ 7/28/12
Justin Mark O'Meara ♥ 10/4/83 ~ 9/6/09
Justin Michael Gregg ♥ 12/03/85 ~ 10/4/10
Justin Ryan Maitland ♥ 8/22/80 ~ 10/7/80
Justin Seebeck ♥ 11/30/87 ~ 3/16/12
Justin Sherrill ♥ 10/25/90 ~ 04/26/12
Justin Stochmal ♥ 1/7/92 ~ 9/1/01
Justin Thomas Ward "JT" ♥ 3/29/89 ~ 5/2/13
Kaely "KK" Nicole Heaven Osterhus ♥ 8/29/05 ~ 4/17/09
Kaelyn Emilia-Hart Callender ♥ 1/14/09 ~ 5/21/10
Kaelyn Marie Rose Low ♥ 2/7/11 ~ 4/10/11
Kai Hartley ♥ 12/27/10
Kaidynce Leona Randolph ♥ 7/1/06
Kaila Marie Harlan ♥ 8/27/91 ~ 8/29/13
Kaili Marie Skeens ♥ 6/30/09 ~ 4/26/10
Kaitlyn Barbara Saenz ♥ 10/04/13
Kaitlyn Nicole Wingate ♥ 9/9/94 ~ 3/25/12
Kaleb Jordan Tutt ♥ 12/7/05
Kaleb Scott Lee Chidester ♥ 7/16/08
Kaleb Wayne ♥ 2/17/11 ~ 3/3/11
Kamberlyn Nicole ♥ 12/27/10
Kami Marie Tutt ♥ 9/23/09
Kamron Edwards ♥ 1/9/06 ~ 7/27/11
Kara Collins ♥ age 26 ~ 1/19/09
Karina Spaulonci ♥ 7/15/85 ~ 2/15/13
Karissa Marie Bermudez ♥ 11/9/08
Kasey Allen Swanger ♥ 2/05/82 ~ 12/18/05
Katelyn and Kristen Polson ♥ 11/30/95
Katey Lester ♥ 8/16/87 ~ 2/14/06
Kathlyn Joy Davis ♥ 7/30/09
Kathy Stiehl-Helms ♥ 1988
Katlyn Elizabeth Brewer ♥ 6/14/92 ~ 5/11/11
Katlynn Marie Smith ♥ 10/8/88
Katrina Diane Spinardi Moore ♥ 8/05/84 ~ 6/05/10
Katrina Moore ♥ 1/9/04
Keely Marie Devine ♥ 3/31/90 ~ 9/7/13
Kelli Marie Douglass ♥ 12/23/59 ~ 5/18/04
Kelly William Cheek ♥ 8/15/69 ~ 12/09/96.
Kelsey MacArthur Hanlan ♥ 5/14/85 ~ 4/14/07
Kelsey Tammy-Jo Norton ♥ 6/5/12

Kelsi-Dione Haffenden ♥ 5/11/01
Kenneth "KC" Hartman Conner ♥ 6/5/94 ~ 1/28/10
Kenneth Charles Russell II ♥ 7/19/83 ~ 1/8/11
Kenneth Jason Currey ♥ 11/5/75 ~ 11/29/99
Kenneth Lee Minks ♥ 8/7/85 ~ 8/26/09
Kenneth Moses ♥ 5/15/80 ~ 8/20/10
Kenneth Wayne McCormick III ♥ 6/24/89 ~ 7/6/12
Kenny Bowen ♥ 1/23/82 ~ 8/7/99.
Kenton Matthew Fults ♥ 11/12/08 ~ 4/1/10
Kerry-louise Bates ♥ 11/16/88 ~ 11/17/88
Kevin Anthony Sanders ♥ 8/09/95 ~ 11/22/10
Kevin F. Baker ♥ 1/7/78 ~ 7/12/05
Kevin Foster Hall ♥
Kevin James Davidson ♥ 8/8/97 ~ 8/3/98
Kevin Lee Crawford ♥ 8/18/89
Kevin Patrick Scullen ♥ 6/3/99
Kevin Thomas Bowles ♥ 2/10/71 ~ 4/4/91
Keyaera Anne Hughey ♥ 4/10/01 ~ 4/17/04
Kiana Sue Sommerville ♥ 12/8/08 ~ 2/24/09
Kieran William Shore ♥ 8/9/10 ~ 9/11/10
Kieren James Norris ♥ 5/10/93
Kimberly Marie Hamilton ♥ 8/14/87 ~ 5/7/04
Kirk Pfister Jr. ♥ 3/3/82 ~ 9/23/13
Kit Darwood ♥ 6/10/83 ~ 10/7/06
Korylette Kucken ♥ 6/29/00 ~ 6/1/11
Krista Leigh Dorsey ♥ 7/24/90 ~ 8/21/05
Kristen Marie Monzon ♥ 11/7/89 ~ 10/25/10
Kristi Hardin ♥ 4/5/93 ~ 4/28/11
Kristi Lee Landini ♥ 7/31/88 ~ 11/26/88
Kristie Lyn Hill ♥ 9/11/80 ~ 6/17/11
Kristy Sue Spicer-Spicer ♥ 3/9/73 ~ 4/5/11
Krystail Champain Yergeau ♥ 3/7/99 ~ 3/7/99
Kurtis Robert Cleaver ♥ 11/16/79 ~ 6/29/04
Kyle Barry John Rutherford ♥ 8/1/06
Kyle Jared Sullivan ♥ 4/29/88 ~ 10/20/09
Kyle Lloyd James ♥ 2/8/90 ~ 10/19/10
Kyle Richard Wene ♥ 6/16/86 ~ 2/8/11
Kyle W. Good ♥ 12/12/92 ~ 1/16 13
Kyran Alidar Liles ♥ 1/25/11 ~ 1/31/11
Landen Everett Epperson ♥ 1/01/99 ~ 9/12/10

Lane Clabough ♥ 2/11/00 ~ 1/24/13
Latesha Lee Mouser ♥ 4/05/88 ~ 1/1/10
Laura Lisa Bingley ♥ 11/23/87 ~ 9/15/08
Laura Lynne Wilson Wechsler ♥ 10/1/07 ~ 10/3/07
Lauren Elizabeth Pacenta ♥ 10/4/88 ~ 11/23/05
Lauren Lillian Robinson ♥ 9/22/10
Laurian Joy Baaske ♥ 2/23/97 ~ 7/04/10
Lawrence Wyatt Lee Fletcher ♥ 3/1/09 ~ 3/29/09
Leah Autumn Schaaf ♥ 9/14/05 ~ 5/1/08
Leeroy Damian De Leon ♥ 3/1/12 ~ 9/30/13
Leif Eric Harris ♥ 7/15/86 ~ 11/16/07
Leo Charles Oliver ♥ 1/30/13 ~ 8/28/13
Lexi Worrell ♥ 4/23/01 ~ 4/8/10
Lilianna Sofi a LaChangita ♥ 2/27/11
Lilyan Cayla Wilson ♥ 1/6/11 ~ 1/29/11
Lindsay Jean Wenzel Lopez ♥ 9/25/78 ~ 11/22/10
Lindsey Mae Maxwell ♥ 11/18/00 ~ 8/19/10
Lisa Elizabeth Goodwin ♥ 11/14/89 ~ 5/18/02
Lisa Jordan ♥ 2/2/74 ~ 5/27/09
Lisa Kay Holdgrafer ♥ 7/2/74 ~ 6/19/05
Lisa Marie Hammers ♥ 3/13/82 ~ 2/5/10
Lisa Michele Duran ♥ 11/26/71 ~ 8/19/07
Lisa Michelle Waring♥ 9/20/86 ~ 11/25/86
Logan Thomas Plant ♥ 6/1/04 ~ 11/17/10
Lorelai Tess Roberts ♥ 4/22/11
Luca Ortenzio ♥ 12/7/12 ~ 2/5/13
Lucas Damian Bortz ♥ 3/01/10 ~ 7/30/10
Lucas James Lafl eur ♥ 6/16/09
Lucas Richard Donnelly ♥ 6/3/11
Luke Howard Pendleton ♥ 7/06/10
Luke Hyslop ♥ 2/27/11 ♥ Angel and Whisper at 12 weeks
Luna Zola Beatty ♥ 4/15/03 ~ 4/16/03
Lydia Marie Greer ♥ 11/27/02 ~ 7/16/08
Lyra Jean' Mitchell ♥ 5/8/10
Macey Jaqeline-Rose Nind ♥ 4/18/11
Mackenzie Jones ♥ 8/22/02 ~ 8/26/02
Maddie Diane Kephart ♥ 2/20/88 ~ 4/29/11
Maddie Thomas ♥ 4/12/90 ~ 11/26/10
Madelyn Elise Buono ♥ 12/27/10
Madison Haley Arnold ♥ 10/01/94 ~ 3/12/09

Maggie Kovski ♥ 5/05 ~ 5/30/07
Maggie Mae Herrick ♥ 11/30/10
Malaikye Thomas Payne ♥ 3/29/10 ~ 8/15/11
Malaki Zane Mangum ♥ 11/20/99
Marc Kenneth Stanton ♥ 12/27/66 ~ 12/15/06
Marcus "Mark" Dean Tyler ♥ 4/19/66 ~ 12/5/92
Mareesa Abrahamson ♥ 4/22/72 ~ 3/01/11
Margaret Amelia Carey Kovski (Maggie) ♥ 5/6/05 ~ 5/30/07
Margaret Ruth Stewart ♥ 6/21/83
Maria Avalon Lovell ♥ 7/28/08 ~ 7/29/08
Marie Stockwell♥ 6/2/92 ~ 2/19/12
Marissa Nicole Olson ♥ 3/24/91 ~ 3/12/13
Mark Allen Gregory Jr. ♥ 1/22/05 ~ 8/13/05
Mark Anthony (Tony) Weber ♥ 6/13/95 ~ 11/27/09
Mark Harrison ♥ 3/10/82 ~ 12/10/11
Mark M. ♥ 11/14/78 ~ 4/3/03
Marley Skillman ♥ 9/25/09 ~ 12/17/10
Martha Rose Elliot ♥ 4/4/11
Marti LoMonaco ♥ 4/16/62 ~ 11/3/09
Mason Alexander Charles Eckhart ♥ 7/16/90 ~ 4/18/09
Mason Alexander Clink ♥ 7/9/11
Mason Jeremiah Wright ♥ 1/30/11
Mason Robert Diehl ♥ 10/18/13 ~ 10/19/13
Mathew Jameson ♥ 8/19/88 ~ 3/25/05
Mathew Wagner ♥ 3/1/94 ~ 7/15/04
Matt Tucker ♥ 12/7/82 ~ 11/19/08
Matthew ♥ 11/16/86 ~ 4/28/07
Matthew Broughton Garrett ♥ 11/20/78 ~ 10/9/10
Matthew Darren Bransden ♥ 2/13/81 ~ 10/12/81
Matthew David Herrera ♥ 5/19/88 ~ 11/10/09
Matthew Dean Hagan ♥ 5/24/85 ~ 4/4/03
Matthew Glenn DeSpain ♥ 6/25/89 ~ 12/13/91
Matthew H Witzgall ♥ 11/24/89 ~ 2/3/11
Matthew Keith Brashear ♥ 12/24/84 ~ 11/4/10
Matthew Liam Rupe ♥ 3/19/04 ~ 3/21/04
Matthew W. McKinnon ♥ 10/24/97 ~ 1/16/11
Maureen Chesebro ♥ 5/3/11
Maurem Marie Douglass ♥ 5/12/61 ~ 7/12/86
Maximus Allen Sevier ♥ 10/7/10 ~ 1/20/11
Meagan-Chante' Jacqualine Everton ♥ 12/8/99 ~ 11/2/11

Megan Ann Thornhill ♥ 3/7/90 ~ 1/28/13
Megan Lauren Major ♥ 2/23/80 ~ 3/8/11
Megan Mahan ♥ 12/04/01 ~ 3/29/13
Mekhail Isaak Mangum ♥ 5/24/00 ~ 6/4/00
Melanie Patricia Bourke ♥ 6/4/85 ~ 12/7/10
Melinda Rose Silva ♥ 5/13/76 ~ 1/6/05
Menetta Fenemor-Halsey ♥ 10/17/05
Merridith J Flick-Burke ♥ 2/16/77 ~ 10/18/01
Meshael Richardson ♥ 6/20/86 ~ 6/18/01
Micah Even Smith ♥ 5/27/07
Michael A. Crafton Jr. ♥ 7/15/04 ~ 8/3/04
Michael Alan Krack ♥ 8/11/99 ~ 6/4/00
Michael Bradley Baker ♥ 10/12/09
Michael D. Crotty ♥ 4/14/83 ~ 4/8/08
Michael Dwain Bradley ♥ 12/30/80 ~ 3/15/11
Michael Flynn ♥ 5/31/87 ~ 4/7/10
Michael Francis Limosani ♥ 12/06/88 ~ 10/26/09
Michael Jordan Svarc ♥ 10/20/84 ~ 4/01/11
Michael McKinley Royal ♥ 4/6/79 ~ 7/3/13
Michael Portaro ♥ 5/25/88 ~ 3/30/11
Michael R. Kern ♥ 4/30/81 ~ 4/13/07
Michael Reynolds ♥ 12/5/86 ~ 1/23/11
Michael Roy Anderson ♥ 10/16/90 ~ 10/17/10
Michael Serrett ♥ 8/21/84 ~ 6/20/10
Michael Steele ♥ 3/26/98 ~ 7/1/13
Michael W. Jackson ♥ 9/26/81 ~ 7/03/05
Micheal James Adkins ♥ 6/16/89 ~ 5/20/12
Micheal James Hammond ♥ 2/1/93 ~ 2/3/93
Micheal S. Wamser ♥ 5/11/87 ~ 12/17/10
Michelle Renee "Chelle" Walker ♥ 5/2/90 ~ 8/31/01
Michial Istre ♥ 6/2/79 ~ 9/2/06
Michial Istre Jr. ♥ 11/11/01 ~ 5/29/10
Mikey James Stokes ♥ 12/24/02 ~ 8/22/09
Mindy Christine Fohl ♥ 4/4/74 ~ 3/20/09
Miracle Faith Williams ♥ 8/17/11 ~ 8/18/11
Miranda Diane Daly ♥ 7/20/84 ~ 8/12/07
Miranda Lynae Boeckman ♥ 1/21/85 ~ 6/9/07
Miranda McFarland ♥ 2/18/89 ~ 2/25/89
Misha Stone ♥ 4/19/90 ~ 4/24/09
Mishale Anna Langston ♥ 9/17/92 ~ 12/6/92

Mitchell "Mitch" Scott Blank ♥ 10/15/66 ~ 7/27/01
Mitchell John Thomas Brennan ♥ 10/17/92 ~ 12/3/10
Monica Bivens ♥ 6/4/90 ~ 5/23/12
NaKeithan Scott Gray ♥ 3/6/10 ~ 5/4/10
Nancy Jane Prater ♥ 2/15/88 ~ 11/18/10
Narin Ramkumar ♥ 11/21/92 ~ 7/1/12
Natalia and Santiago Hernandez-Swain ♥ 8/07/09
Natalia Canales ♥ 5/14/11
Natalie Kathryn Johnson ♥ 3/30/98 ~ 12/1/09
Natallie Sue Kay Daugherty ♥ 6/10/11
Natasha Whitmore ♥ 1979 ~ 2007
Natassia Pereira Da Silva ♥ 8/1/83 ~ 8/29/07
Nathan Andrew Young ♥ 9/19/88 ~ 6/22/08
Nathan Bradley Lawrence ♥ 1/29/85 ~ 6/24/11
Nathan David Stratton ♥ 2/14/11 ~ 5/10/11
Nathan Lee Westberry ♥ 10/24/05
Nathaniel Matthew Payne ♥ 6/25/99 ~ 9/21/13
Naudia Fornfeist ♥ 12/27/10 ~ 2/12/11
Nayan Chandra ♥ 4/18/80 ~ 5/17/85
Naythan Maina ♥ 1/17/11
Nevaeh Hope Sousa ♥ 7/18/10 ~ 7/28/10
Nevaeh Neema ♥ 11/07/13 ~ 4/9/13
Niccolas Fogarty ♥ 7/8/91
Nicholas "Nic" Muir ♥ 6/25/87 ~ 4/13/07
Nicholas Alexander Arnold ♥ 6/26/01 ~ 11/7/02
Nicholas Isaiah Imler ♥ 7/29/76
Nicholas J. Marro III ♥ 8/31/82 ~ 10/9/10
Nicholas W. Swift (Nick) ♥ 9/29/93 ~ 8/15/12
Nicholas Wayne Steele ♥ 5/19/90 ~ 6/22/90
Nick Shelton ♥
Nickolas W. Eickenroth ♥ 6/2/88 ~ 8/10/05
Nicola Jane Perry ♥ 7/22/88 ~ 1/23/89
Nicole Byrd ♥ 3/28/93 ~ 8/19/96
Nicole Christine Bohlmeier ♥ 9/28/79 ~ 9/21/97
Nicole Marie Brown ♥ 3/28/89 ~ 1/1/07
Nicole Marie Klika ♥ 9/9/83 ~ 9/15/83
Nikolai Alexander McClain "Little Steven" ♥ 3/20/95 ~ 9/8/13
Nikolas Ryan Chunn ♥ 2/21/02 ~ 8/18/07
Noah Cooper French ♥ 7/15/11
Noah Fogarty ♥ 7/5/00

Noah Markiewicz ♥ 9/30/12 ~ 8/17/13
Noah Michael Mann ♥ 2/12/73 ~ 2/17/10
Nolan Michael Dowaliby ♥ 6/8/09 ~ 6/11/09
Nora Elizabeth Grothe ♥ 3/6/01
Nsuku Ndlovu ♥ 3/20/93 ~ 9/20/11
Ocean Rose ♥ 10/31/13
Oliver Murphy ♥ 4/18/11
Oliver Thompson ♥ 3/3/09 ~ 10/21/09
Oscar Charlie Oldfield-Archer ♥ 4/21/08
Osclie Oscar Oldfield-Archer ♥ 4/12/08
Owen Michael James Downes ♥ 1/15/01 ~ 6/2/01
Owen Walsh ♥ 6/12/10 ~ 6/13/10
P.J. Bueno ♥ 7/25/84 ~ 11/15/07
Paige Helen McCoy ♥ 4/1/08
Pamela Jolene Norman ♥ 4/24/80 ~ 3/2/06
Patricia "Trishie Bubbles" Ann Murray ♥ 4/7/84 ~ 7/12/10
Patrick "Charlie" Kelly Jr. ♥ 3/16/70 ~ 7/11/99
Patrick David Holley ♥ 2/14/81 ~ 2/13/10
Patrick Russell Caprino ♥ 2/20/69 ~ 10/20/12
Patrick Spencer Silbitzer ♥ 10/6/85 ~ 11/18/09
Patrisha (Trisha) Lee Ann Osipovitch ♥ 2/11/77 ~ 1/15/95
Patty Burgdoff ♥ 7/6/98 ~ 12/8/06
Paul G. Babloski Jr. ♥ 6/4/90 ~ 10/1/09
Paul Joseph Mithcell ♥ 9/29/47 ~ 2/23/69
Paul Wm. Schumacher ♥ 3/10/84 ~ 8/31/05
Pauline Michelle Craig ♥ 1/6/70 ~ 10/6/85
Philip Allan Walter Tognola ♥ 3/1/98 ~ 4/19/03
Phillip "PJ" Bueno Jr. ♥ 7/25/84 ~ 11/15/07
Phillip McFarland ♥ 8/18/93 ~ 11/5/12
Phillipa Campbell ♥ 11/3/89 ~ 8/28/09
Pip Connor ♥ 2/4/11
Poppy Ann Rudkin ♥ 7/11/10
Preston R. Madison ♥ 8/20/06 ~ 5/30/10
Princess Sienna Mary Rees ♥ 11/17/09
Priya Anjali Chandra ♥ 1/13/86 ~ 2/10/89
Quinton Liam Wallace ♥ 6/1/11
Rachael Ellen Thompson ♥ 11/5/81 ~ 6/26/08
Rachel Plog ♥ 4/18/90 ~ 12/8/06
Rain Serenity Arizola ♥ 10/20/07
Ramon M. Gallegos Jr. ♥ 11/24/80 ~ 11/27/10

Randi Mae ♥ 10/1/92 ~ 10/1/92
Randy Spurlock ♥ 5/3/71 ~ 1/10/11
Raymond A. Bryan IV ♥ 1/27/87 ~ 9/17/07
Raymond Benjamin Moppin Jr. ♥ 5/1/09 ~ 7/29/09
Rebecca and Rachel Tardif ♥ 3/11/04
Rebecca Anne Norris ♥ 10/10/79 ~ 9/12/09
Rebecca Louise Bosdyk ♥ 1/3/83
Rebecca Marie Peterson ♥ 7/6/89 ~ 9/30/07
Reed Alexander Cantler ♥ 10/23/96 ~ 12/22/10
Reed Joseph Kelsey ♥ 4/15/93 ~ 4/5/07
Ren and Simply ♥ 2/14/11
Rey of Hope Lucero ♥ 6/19/10
Ricardo E. Ignacio ♥ 1/8/87 ~ 7/9/07
Richard "Rick" Allen Fudge ♥ 1/3/84 ~ 10/24/85
Richard "Ricky" Scott Schumann ♥ 6/3/86 ~ 2/21/10
Richard Scott King ♥ 1/8/90 ~ 1/10/09
Richard Sylvester ♥ 11/1/85 ~ 11/1/06
Richard-John Alexander Akon Roberts ♥ 2/24/10
Ricky D. Lanham ♥ 9/21/79 ~ 12/23/10
Ricky Love ♥ 2/11/77 ~ 1/17/05
Ridgway "Ridge" Westin Blackburn ♥ 4/3/11
River Esparza Dougherty ♥ 4/27/98
Rob Niebieski ♥ 3/30/71 ~ 5/19/11
Robbie Gambrell ♥ 10/7/69 ~ 6/16/94
Robbie Mitchell ♥ 5/26/85 ~ 1/10/09
Robbie Robert David Speer ♥ 8/12/85 ~ 9/15/08
Robby Nelson ♥ 9/16/82 ~ 10/17/09
Robert "Bobby" Lee Kasch ♥ 7/17/80 ~ 5/19/06
Robert "Robbie" James Gambrel III ♥ 10/7/69 ~ 6/16/94
Robert Allen Hunt ♥ 4/14/86 ~ 1/16/11
Robert Fred (LB) Taylor ♥ 12/3/90 ~ 4/23/13
Robert Hanson Jr. ♥ 1/26/82 ~ 7/16/10
Robert John Clark II and Keith Raymond Clark ♥ 5/7/1972
Robert Joseph Cooper ♥ 4/12/73 ~ 5/30/95
Robert Layton ♥ 11/26/78 ~ 9/27/09
Robert Lee Hailes ♥ 4/2/88 ~ 7/12/06
Robert Mason Brewer ♥ 6/4/83 ~ 5/4/10.
Robert Raymond Huerta ♥ 9/29/76 ~ 7/7/00
Rocky Allan Lindley ♥ 8/28/83 ~ 10/19/07
Roger Dale Sanders ♥ 10/20/83 ~ 2/6/11

Roger Stiehl ♥ 2001
Rogerlee Staley II"BUBBY " ♥ 9/23/82 ~ 1/22/03
Roman Zac Craven-Phillips ♥ 5/3/09
Ronald "Ronnie" Allen Fraga ♥ 7/7/90 ~ 1/12/08
Ronald Landman ♥ 1/30/88 ~ 10/26/13
Ronnie Juett 3rd ♥ 3/14/84 ~ 9/7/05
Rory Lee Post ♥ 1/7/11 ~ 3/7/11
Russell Neil Coatsworth ♥ 10/25/81 ~ 6/10/09
Rusty Creepingbear ♥ 8/4/78 ~ 10/29/07
Rusty Hyitt ♥ 11/15/81 ~ 7/10/10
Ryan Andrew McGee ♥ 7/2/93 ~ 8/11/13
Ryan Blake Dunn ♥ 5/24/89 ~ 7/16/10
Ryan Dominic DeAndrea ♥ 7/22/82 ~ 3/16/05
Ryan Gene Johnson ♥ 6/16/13
Ryan James McPhee ♥ 10/6/83 ~ 7/8/10
Ryan Keith Harbuck ♥ 6/22/88 ~ 7/21/13
Ryan Michael Savidge ♥ 11/6/85 ~ 11/24/11
Ryan Nicholas Hunt ♥ 5/19/86 ~ 4/24/10
Ryland Cameron Stewart Swayze ♥ 6/9/07 ~ 5/20/10
Ryleigh Jade Karol ♥ 3/31/13
Ryleigh Jayne Wright ♥ 4/24/06
Salvatore Marchese ♥ 4/11/84 ~ 9/23/10
Sam Edward Garrison ♥ 8/29/10 ~ 3/22/11
Sam Moore ♥ 4/22/92 ~ 6/14/12
Samantha Downs ♥ 9/4/88 ~ 10/6/07
Samantha Lauren Martin ♥ 6/4/93 ~ 12/3/06
Samantha Lynn Puhr ♥ 5/24/90 ~ 11/11/11
Samantha Lynn Vogel ♥ 11/03/90 ~ 11/20/11
Samantha Rose Cleghorn ♥ 12/14/10
Sami Summers ♥ 11/16/79 ~ 3/19/99
Samira Joy Nukho ♥ 9/1/83 ~ 5/25/05
Samson Paul Lohaus Fast ♥ 10/15/10
Samual Thomas Smith ♥ 9/16/97 ~ 4/5/11
Samuel Watson ♥ 5/14/03 ~ 8/23/09
Samuel-John Wilson ♥ 1/4/10 ~ 9/4/10
Sara Brielle Knopick ♥ 6/25/08 ~ 8/8/08
Sara Elyse Eastley ♥ 10/7/87 ~ 10/8/10
Sarah E Kraemer ♥ 5/18/82 ~ 8/30/13
Sarah Elizabeth Logan ♥ 3/7/11
Sarah Lisa Guerrero ♥ 10/21/89 ~ 11/16/06

Sarah Natalia Salsano ♥ 11/19/05
Sarah Nichole Andricks ♥ 1/12/83 ~ 1/25/95
Sariah McKenzie Best ♥ 11/21/08 ~ 2/18/09
Savanah Marie Whitney ♥ 12/18/09 ~ 2/15/10
Savannah Elaine Berumen-Owens ♥ 5/24/11
Savannah Leigh Hart ♥ 4/4/94 ~ 1/19/97
Savannah Mahan ♥ 9/11/97 ~ 3/29/13
Scarlett Payne ♥ 1/3/09
Scarlette Adora ♥ 12/20/10 ~ 6/6/11
Scott A. Schwartz Jr. ♥ 9/2/85 ~ 4/20/07
Scott Allen Reece ♥ 3/8/73 ~ 8/5/10
Scott David Walz ♥ 9/12/91 ~ 3/4/10
Scott Duncan ♥ 8/5/79 ~ 4/12/09
Sean Alexander Turanicza ♥ 9/9/92 ~ 4/7/12
Sean Charles Grubbs ♥ 7/18/78 ~ 5/12/07
Serena Peyton Tasker ♥ 2/17/00 ~ 3/14/11
Serenity Grace Kushman ♥ 6/10/10
Sergio Hyland ♥ 5/28/02 ~ 8/6/04
Shannon Markiewicz ♥ 3/24/99 ~ 4/20/99
Sharonrose Gudu ♥ 7/2/12 ~ 10/19/12
Shaun David Hedstrom ♥ 11/14/81 ~ 5/11/13
Shawn Michael Broadus ♥ 6/5/87 ~ 4/11/06
Shawn Preston Rego ♥ 5/29/90 ~ 3/22/06
Shayla M. Aston ♥ 9/16/04 ~ 5/8/09
Shaylee Mikah Mangum ♥ 10/24/01
Shayna Alise Casilla ♥ 3/28/05
Shelbie Werth ♥ 10/5/94 ~ 6/6/11
Shelby Thomas McCorkle ♥ 8/27/00 ~ 3/6/11
Sheyenne Lynne Chappell ♥ 7/15/06
Shianna M. Aston ♥ 9/17/02 ~ 7/8/09
Sinead Morley-Shephard ♥ 7/12/06
Skyler DeShawn Bradley Priester ♥ 3/29/08 ~ 5/10/08
Sophee Olivia Widner ♥ 11/23/10 ~ 6/12/11
Sophia Grace Velazquez ♥ 5/31/11
Sophie Isabella Torrens ♥ 1/22/09 ~ 4/2/09
Spencer Matthew Jordan ♥ 9/30/05 ~ 10/25/05
Stacy Noel Sobieski ♥ 3/18/82 ~ 5/30/05
Stann Justice Davis ♥ 5/15/11
Stephen Anthony ♥ 2/15/11
Stephen Benjamin McClarence ♥ 4/23/87 ~ 2/6/89

Stephen Jon Ellenberger ♥ 7/16/91 ~ 4/1/08
Stephen LaSorsa ♥ 2/17/80 ~ 1/2/06
Stephen Tyler Dobbins ♥ 6/2/91 ~ 11/16/96
Sterling Snow Kushman ♥ 1/6/11
Steven Christopher Mills ♥ 9/15/92 ~ 5/22/10
Steven Eugene Handy II ♥ 2/3/02 ~ 7/18/02
Steven Lee Anglebrandt ♥ 12/27/87 ~ 7/23/07
Steven Lownie ♥ 5/30/84 ~ 10/7/07
Steven Mathis ♥ 1/31/74 ~ 5/15/04
Steven Michael Johnson ♥ 1/28/89 ~ 10/24/07
Steven Patrick Miller ♥ 8/31/84 ~ 3/31/06
Stewart Ian Reed ♥ 3/20/89 ~ 1/17/09
Sydney Anne Evans ♥ 10/19/07 ~ 11/28/09
Tabitha Renee' Drum ♥ 9/23/92 ~ 10/1/92
Tabitha Ruby Garay ♥ 12/31/01 ~ 7/9/12
Talia Rosaly Leombruno ♥ 10/18/10 ~ 2/07/11
Tamika Judith Short ♥ 12/3/95 ~ 12/5/05
Tammy Logan ♥ 9/17/90 ~ 2/5/91
Taylor Marie Vaughan ♥ 9/20/97 ~ 6/10/09
Taylor Noel Todora ♥ 1/15/87 ~ 6/18/07
Taylor Tropio ♥ 11/15/94 ~ 7/2/11
Taylor Vignes ♥ 1/15/87 ~ 6/18/07
Teagan Chloe Curtis ♥ 9/26/06 ~ 9/3/09
Teagan E. Dickenson ♥ 7/5/97 ~ 3/8/00
Teagan Eugene Paxton ♥ 9/20/06 ~ 11/26/06
Teara Renee Stokes Hagood ♥ 8/12/79 ~ 1/14/08
Tegan-Rose Major ♥ 5/31/07
Teresa Kay Lebo ♥ 9/13/06 ~ 3/17/07
Thomas Alan Losty ♥ 12/8/10
Thomas Joseph Ramsden ♥ 8/14/90 ~ 8/1/91
Thomas Joseph Serewicz Sr. ♥ 10/11/85 ~ 7/17/10
Thomas Lynn ♥ 8/31/02
Thomas Mathew Tucker ♥ 12/7/82 ~ 11/19/08
Thomas Wenzel Culver ♥ 9/6/75 ~ 6/26/02
Tiara Segrist ♥ 9/27/89 ~ 6/12/11
Tierra Rae Pierson ♥ 7/17/98 ~ 12/19/10
Tiffany Marie Gallo ♥ 3/23/87 ~ 6/25/11
Timmy Thompson ♥ 6/3/77 ~ 4/18/04
Timothy "Jason" Jones ♥ 5/24/09 ~ 10/31/09
Timothy Connors ♥ 7/26/95 ~ 5/17/11

Timothy E. Boutelle ♥ 5/10/89 ~ 7/28/10
Timothy Kyle Owens ♥ 10/24/77 ~ 6/24/11
Timothy Lee Nickos ♥ 6/12/94 ~ 6/28/11
Timothy Scott Hall ♥ 5/19/85 ~ 7/17/06
Timothy Thomas Moye ♥ 9/16/79 ~ 3/13/03
Tina Marie Elizabeth Gaither ♥ 9/20/95 ~ 11/10/98
Tina Michelle Lawson-Hutchens ♥ 2/25/83 ~ 4/24/03
Tiny Lux Lopez ♥ 3/9/10
Tomas Reece Morris-Welch ♥ 1/21/05
Tommy Bennett ♥ 9/18/99 ~ 11/25/03
Tommy Drake Randolph ♥ 8/24/07 ~ 4/28/08
Tommy Lee Baum ♥ 9/8/04 ~ 10/8/04
Tommy M. Childress ♥ 6/30/87 ~ 8/4/05
Toni Ann Hales ♥ 6/4/90 ~ 11/3/05
Tony Mahan ♥ 5/24/74 ~ 3/29/13
Tony Sansome ♥ 4/19/71~ 12/8/00
Tori Lee Cantu ♥ 2/17/97 ~ 4/14/10
Tracey Faye Pellegrini ♥ 10/27/74 ~ 1/11/08
Tracy Ann Gavel ♥ 1/25/74 ~ 10/9/88
Travis John Allen Carnes Sr. ♥ 12/19/86 ~ 12/5/12
Travis W. Mortimer ♥ 5/26/86 ~ 1/13/12
Trenton Cole Bailey-Stout ♥ 11/18/91 ~ 10/20/05
Trenton Lee Newlon ♥ 1/12/95 ~ 7/15/08
Trevor Wayne Jones ♥ 6/11/79 ~ 2/8/09
Treyton J. Whaley ♥ 9/24/06
Trinity Nicole Wright ♥ 1/11/10 ~ 2/22/10
Trisha Anne P. Dionisio ♥ 6/9/00 ~ 9/1/13
Ty Nichols ♥ 2/1/92 ~ 6/21/08
Ty Stevens ♥ 1/27/97 ~ 3/15/11
Tyler Boudreaux ♥ 7/28/89 ~ 4/16/09
Tyler Davis Lampman ♥ 7/27/96 ~ 10/19/09
Tyler Edward Dawdy ♥ 2/22/89 ~ 5/19/07
Tyler Paul Lippstreu ♥ 11/26/89 ~ 7/1/12
Tyler Ray Parmenter ♥ 9/4/72 ~ 3/30/02
Tyler Shane Richardson ♥ 8/14/04 ~10/3/06
Tyson Lee Shingledecker Coburn ♥ 7/7/10 ~ 3/14/11
Vallerina Jeanette Ramos ♥ 5/12/88 ~ 7/22/88
Veronica Jane Oulch ♥ 5/7/81 ~ 10/2/11
Vicky Leanne Johnson ♥ 8/31/03
Vito E. Pistone IV ♥ 10/22/81 ~ 7/10/10

Walter Timothy Cohen ll ♥ 8/14/89 ~ 1/25/10
Warren V. White ♥ 1/24/03 ~ 4/23/11
Waylon Andrew McDonald ♥ 10/2/81 ~ 10/14/12
Wendy Sunderlin ♥ 6/18/77 ~ 11/12/96
Wesley Dustin Imler Sr. ♥ 6/3/77 ~ 8/29/05
Wesley Hunter Yackle ♥ 8/05/03 ~ 6/03/06
Wesley Wayne Phillips ♥ 3/10/81 ~ 7/23/08
William "Billy" King ♥ 12/14/90 ~ 11/9/08
William David Hawkins♥ 3/20/02
William Durasky ♥ 4/30/87 ~ 12/2/12
William Gaines Lowe ♥ 7/27/10
William Hart ♥ 5/2/07
William James Sansalone ♥ 5/24/95 ~ 7/29/05
William M. Harkanson ♥ 10/30/85 ~ 2/23/88
William Mullis (Daniel) ♥ 8/17/89 ~ 5/13/12
William S. Carney ♥ 7/17/80 ~ 6/5/04
Willow Kyliegh Loralye Chapman ♥ 1/22/11
Wyatt Dillon Caviglia ♥ 12/28/08 ~ 2/2/11
Wyatt Miracle Lee ♥ 12/9/07 ~ 4/7/08
Xandrea Jolean Cruz ♥ 9/10/02 ~ 10/11/02
Xavier Michael King ♥ 1/27/98 ~ 6/6/11
Xavier Ricky-Allan Tanswell ♥ 11/16/10
Xzavier Alan Francisco ♥ 4/14/03 ~ 5/29/11
Yasovardhan Thakur ♥ 4/25/90 ~ 12/15/11
Zachariah Dennis Marsh ♥ 8/27/95 ~ 10/5/07
Zachariah Moore ♥ 7/13/08 ~ 7/25/08
Zachary Aaron Smith ♥ 3/20/82 ~ 6/18/03
Zachary Allen Thacker ♥ 2/25/86 ~ 9/23/10
Zachary Bynum ♥ 10/17/94 ~ 1/7/13
Zachary Devon Shafer ♥ 2/19/08 ~ 12/8/08
Zachary James Cook ♥ 7/2/92 ~ 11/8/09
Zachery Murdock ♥ 3/3/96 ~ 2/2/13
Zachry Thomas Patrician ♥ 9/1/95 ~ 8/25/13
Zackary Matthew Bell ♥ 1/12/01 ~ 6/13/01
Zahra Belle Benboubaddi ♥ 6/28/11
Zakk Anthony Devlin ♥ 8/11/09
Zane Reagan Draycott ♥ 1/06
Zina Ann Manuel Pitts ♥ 11/14/63 ~ 11/2/13
Zineb Beatrice Benboubaddi ♥ 6/29/11
Zoe Ann Lawhon ♥ 5/6/11 ~ 5/6/11

Zoe Isabella Lemmons ♥ 10/31/10
Zoe Maree Wait ♥ 2/23/81 ~ 7/26/04
Zoey Mae Rea ♥ 6/21/12
Zoey Rae-Leigh Hawkins ♥ 3/11/03
Zoey Renee Elizabeth Lin Smith ♥ 12/29/01 ~ 4/12/04
Zoie Nina Woods ♥ 11/9/10

EPILOGUE BY J.T. BAPTISTA

I told my mom I wanted to write the epilogue since this book was such an inspirational experience for her. She healed in so many ways by writing this book and she now knows she can accomplish anything. She would be ashamed to admit the number of times she wanted to quit. So much pushed her on, including me, but there were times she really felt so overwhelmed by the enormity of what she was doing that it got the best of her. I told her she is an inspiration to others, but she just laughs.

My point in writing this is to tell all of you the same thing. We all come from the same place, which is where I am now. You know your loved ones are happy just by the feeling you get when they visit! We are so happy here. That does not mean we have forgotten you or will not be there when you call on us. We love to help you in any way we can and will be the first to jump and cheer for you when you have reached a goal or overcome something you didn't think you could overcome.

We are also here to help push you in the direction you need to go to make the most out of the life you have. Many of you do not feel very accomplished or supported. We want this to change. This book is the first step to a new life for you! If you are reading this epilogue, that probably means you made it this far! Don't stop here, please! We want you to go beyond the reaches of your mind and soar with us to the highest of highs. What does that mean? It means you need to be diligent in your work with us. We didn't drag you all the way here just to have you turn around and say, "It's too hard" or "I'm not good enough" or "Why would my child want to come back to help me?" From where we stand, that is all rubbish! I've always wanted to say that word. Rubbish!

My mom has proven you can do whatever you set your mind to do. Don't let anything stand in the way of learning more about where we are now and what we are doing. We are so excited to share this and so much more with you. We will always be your children— always. We are also so much more than that, if you haven't already figured that out. Please reach out to us and trust we will be there when you call, because we will!

My mom had to make the commitment to learn how to talk with me. You need to make the commitment to learn how to talk to your child, or your dad or mom or sister or brother. Now that you know it is possible, what is stopping you? Nothing? Good!

I am here to help you, too. If you need me, call on me. I go by J.T. up here, so call me and I will come help in whatever way you need. You have entered a different world by reading this book, a world you will enjoy more than you know.

A word about those in your life who might not support your connection with your child or loved one: Listen to your heart. Your heart knows what is right for you. Others might feel they know, but their fears might be getting in the way of their own learning. My mom had to work through a lot of this as she was learning how to communicate with me, but she never gave up and never let others' fears hold her back. She knew it really was me talking to her. She knew it in the depths of her heart. I invite you to do the same. Check in with your heart to see. The heart never lies.

My mom can help you if you need it. She's one amazing woman! I am so glad she is my mom!

Thank you for reading this. Now get to work!

ABOUT THE AUTHOR

Sarina Baptista is an internationally renowned psychic medium, mentor, author and speaker. She was a featured speaker for the "Life, Death and Beyond" International Conference in Crete, Greece, and is the resident psychic for Clear Channel's Big Country 97.9FM in Northern Colorado. Her clients include adults and children from all areas of the world, including Australia, Italy, India and the UK. Her purpose is to connect us to our angels, guides and loved ones, and teach us how to access this information on our own.

Sarina discovered her gifts through her own tragedy—the passing of her seven-year-old son in March 2007. She learned her son did not really die. He was still very close, leading her to her incredible mediumship gifts. Knowing her son is happy and close by whenever she calls to him made such a difference in her grief recovery.

Sarina works with a collective of Ascended Masters who can see what her clients need and assists in each session. She has created several mediumship training programs, including one on one mentoring, long distance training, workshops and webinars to train others to connect with the other side based upon what she has learned from her son and the Ascended Masters. She holds monthly live events and development workshops demonstrating how we are all connected.

Sarina is also the Psychic Investigator Team Lead for Third Eye Paranormal Investigators, a Northern Colorado paranormal team, and educates home and business owners about these "residents" in their space.

She currently resides in Loveland, Colorado, with her husband, three children, dog and cats. J.T. calls her work "The Bridge to Healing: Connecting Heart and Soul."

For more information about Sarina, please visit http://www.sarinabaptista.com.

RESOURCES

Recommended Reading

Baptista, Sarina *A Bridge to Healing: J.T.'s Story Companion Workbook – A Guide to Connecting to the Other Side*. Loveland: Bridge to Healing Press, 2013

Bolton, Iris *My Son…My Son, A Guide to Healing after Death, Loss or Suicide*. Atlanta: Bolton Press, 1991.

Choquette, Sonia *Ask Your Guides*. Carlsbad: Hay House, 2006.

Holland, John *Power of the Soul: Inside Wisdom for an Outside World*. Carlsbad: Hay House, 2008.

Newton, Michael Ph.D. *Journey of Souls: Case Studies of Life Between Lives*. Woodbury:Llewellyn Publications, 1994.

Van Praagh, James *Growing Up In Heaven*. New York: HarperCollins, 2011.

Weiss, Brian, MD. *Many Lives, Many Masters*. New York: Simon and Schuster, Inc., 1988.

Wolfelt, Alan Ph.D. *Understanding Your Grief: Ten Essential Touchstones for Finding Hope and Healing Your Heart*. Fort Collins: Companion Press, 2003

Websites

http://www.sarinabaptista.com
My website has grief information, resources and more information on how to connect with your loved ones, angels and guides

http://www.johnholland.com/
John Holland's website has very valuable information on
mediumship. His weekly newsletter is also full of great
information and tips to tapping into your psychic self.

http://www.centerforloss.com
Dr. Alan Wolfelt's extensive website for grief, loss and
transition. He has books on every type of loss. He understands
the pain and how to get to the other side of it.

Meditation CDs

Bridge to Healing Connecting Meditations available at
www.sarinabaptista.com

Meditation: Achieving Inner Peace and Tranquility In Your Life — a
book with a CD by Brian Weiss, M.D.

Connecting with Your Animal Spirit Guide — by Steven Farmer

Psychic Navigator: Harnessing Your Inner Guidance — a book with a
CD by John Holland

LETTER TO NEWLY BEREAVED PARENTS

"You will survive this. It might feel like you won't right now, but you will." Those were the words told to me by a lady at my son's viewing. I later learned that her four year old son died about nine years prior. You never would have known it. I asked her in the following weeks, "Are you happy? I mean really happy?" She knew what I meant. You feel like there will never be another happy day, another smile, another joy. She said, "Yes, I am. Of course, there are days when I am not, but most of the time now, I am."

I hung onto those words with all my hope and strength. I knew that she had been heaven-sent and that she would lead me to happiness again, or at the very least, to a day when I could smile at my other children, who so desperately needed me.

I am now almost five years on this journey. I can say with a full heart that I am happy again. I have found joy again. This happened not by running away from my grief, but by falling into it. I had to fall into that deep darkness. I tried to escape it, but it just made it worse. So I succumbed. I learned fairly quickly that by succumbing to it, giving in, as horrible and frightening as it was to be in that pit, I was not there alone. There were many others there with me – other family who had met J.T. when he passed from here to heaven, the many angels who hold us up when we feel like we just cannot take another breath, and, of course, God. God, Source, the Universe, the One, was there in that pit, too. I didn't recognize this until much later, but now looking back, I know they were all holding my head above the muck.

I cannot explain it very well, but I keep trying because I really want other parents to understand this. It is only by truly *being* in your grief that you are able to rise above it. I found that each time I would feel that wave come over me, I would just let go and let it carry me wherever it may. Sooner and sooner, I was carried to the top of the pit, able to climb out and breathe again. We humans don't like to be "uncomfortable." We don't like to be in pain. Losing a child blows that all out of the water. There's nowhere else for us to go. We *have* to be in the pain. Try to not run from it, escape it, numb it or postpone it. It will just come back again. You must deal with it.

I've learned so much since J.T. left, and I wanted to share it with you. I am on the other side of that pain. I *did* survive, and I *did* make it. You can, too. Life will never be the same without your child here, but you *can* make a new life, a new normal, and truly function.

Be easy on yourself. Don't expect anything from yourself for at least a year. Do what you can for your other children, as much as you can give, and don't feel guilty about not being able to engage with them or stop their hurt. It just doesn't work that way. Their grieving is different than yours and they may need professional help down the road. I put both of my children into grief counseling -- one was fine and we stopped the counseling, the other one is still going and probably will for some time. The biggest lesson is to not think it's your responsibility. You have a lot to deal with yourself.

Take all the help you can get right now. I had people offering to clean my bathrooms. Ordinarily, I would have said "No," but it made that person offering feel like he or she was doing something for me. This is not the time for pride, so please take the offers. It makes others feel like they are doing something for you when they have no idea how else to help.

I want you to also know something very important. Our children do bring us signs that they are alright. Watch for them, but try to not obsess on them. Sometimes, grieving parents try to look too hard and then miss the obvious ones, like a butterfly landing on your shoulder, or pennies and feathers in random places in the house. You might hear "Mom" spoken in your child's voice, look around and no one is there. That really is your child, and he or she wants you to know they are just fine. They are not truly gone, as I have learned in depth since J.T. left, and they will not leave us.

Right now, it is your child's job to see you through this. So take the signs and hold them in your heart. Know they are real.

Don't second guess yourself. These gifts will get you through those tough nights when everyone leaves and goes back to their normal lives. In the beginning, I had to have someone come sit with me at night. I called them my "mommy sitters." I was terrified to have the house quiet. I would have panic attacks, and I never had them before. I had plenty of these those first few months. Don't think you are being "weak" or not dealing with things if you have to have someone come over to talk with you, or just watch the kids while you have a meltdown. It is part of this wilderness we are in now. There are no rights and there are no wrongs. Don't judge yourself thinking you should be farther along, or "why this again?" It just is.

I wanted to say a couple of things about siblings. I received so much advice on what to do and what not to do with my children as far as "letting them see you cry" or "keeping them from the pain." I learned some very important things. First, you do need to let them see you cry initially. I found, though, that after the first month, they kept trying to comfort me and wanted to take away my grief, which is definitely not something a child should have to do. So I spent more time at the cemetery without them. It's a great place to scream, yell, beat the ground, throw things, etc., but not have the kids see you do it. I don't want to say to hide your grief from them, because they know more than we think they do. I did have to limit it, though. Your children might be different. You will know what is best so go with your instincts and forget what everyone else says.

Whether we wanted it or not, we are on this road. There are many of us on this road and we hold onto each other with all our strength and hope. We are all at different stages of this journey. There are many who feel they are helping by sharing their stories with you, but you may find it just brings you down. It's alright to limit that kind of support. They mean well, but sometimes it would leave me more depressed than when you came in! Do what you feel is right.

You are loved. You are loved by many in your community, by your child, by God, Source, the Universe, the One. You did not do anything to deserve this. It is not a punishment. I know this for a fact. There is meaning in this, and even though you cannot find it right now, know it is there. You may find that meaning one day, or you may not. This tragedy has nothing to do with judgment, condemnation, past sins, etc. I hope you know that. You are loved, and you are never alone. In the depth of the pain, I know you will feel that hand reach down to you, those arms holding you, just like I did. Hang onto that love, and know that it is real.

My family and I are praying for you, with all our hearts.

ENDNOTES

[1] Averages taken from data from the CDC for 2005, 2006, 2007, 2008 and 2009. Table 1. Deaths and death rates by age, sex, and race and Hispanic origin, and age-adjusted death rates, by sex and race and Hispanic origin: United States, preliminary 2008 and 2009, page 9

[2] Alan Wolfelt, Ph.D. *Understanding Your Grief: Ten Essential Touchstones for Finding Hope and Healing Your Heart.* Fort Collins: Companion Press, 2003

[3] Excerpted from http://en.wikipedia.org/wiki/Synchronicity